Five Essential Competencies of Effective Diversity, Equity, & Inclusion Leaders

Whitney White

2021 Edition

Copyright © 2021 by Whitney White

All rights reserved. This book or any portion thereof may not be reproduced or used in any manner whatsoever without the express written permission of the author and publisher except for the use of brief quotations in a book review.

Printed in the United States of America

Second Printing, December 2021.

Whitney White
WhitneyWhite05@gmail.com

This guidebook is branded under the TalNet IncludeAll initiative that is working to advance diversity, equity, and inclusion in West Michigan. The IncludeAll initiative is one of the five TalNet innovations funded by the Doug and Maria DeVos Foundation.

The information contained within this guidebook should not be construed as legal advice in any manner and specifically within employment and labor law. The authors of this document are not lawyers. Practitioners should seek the advice of legal counsel whenever appropriate to ensure that activities undertaken as part of this guidebook are consistent with local, state, and federal law.

Preface

Business has been a field of study for centuries. The first MBA was issued by the Harvard Graduate School of Business Administration in 1908.

Within the field of business, however, diversity, equity, and inclusion (DE&I) are relatively modern concepts that only recently have received much-needed attention.

The growing emphasis on DE&I has been driven in part by a heightened awareness — by customers, employees, shareholders, and the public — of historic inequities in social systems, including employment.

At the same time, employers themselves increasingly recognize that diversity, equity, and inclusion are essential objectives, not only from a moral standpoint, but also for organizational success.

DE&I is simply good for business, and the return on investment is significant.

This awakening has been evident in West Michigan, where employers have demonstrated their willingness to affirm their commitment to advancing DE&I. This is progress, but it leaves the business community facing a question: How can DE&I commitments be transformed into effective strategies and sustainable efforts?

By building on the foundation established by experienced DE&I leadership, this guide seeks to support the progress of diversity, equity, and inclusion efforts in West Michigan and beyond.

The guide was informed by West Michigan DE&I officers who are recognized for their expertise, credibility, and accomplishments. They contributed their insights to support DE&I progress for West Michigan, but the content is applicable beyond the region.

The most advanced organizations understand that progress in this field requires leadership. That is the purpose of this guide: to document the knowledge, skills, abilities, and other characteristics a DE&I leader needs to drive organizational change. These are examined as five key competencies:

1 Personal Characteristics
Several factors that collectively provide the ability to develop and foster meaningful relationships.

2 Knowledge
Having foundational understanding of DE&I and a commitment to continuous learning.

3 Planning
The ability to envision an ideal future state and develop a plan to achieve it.

4 Leading
The ability to influence people and systems to move organizations forward.

5 Communication
The ability to receive and share information in a number of formats with a wide range of audiences.

The development of this guide illustrated that effective DE&I leaders share not only these competencies but the expertise for putting them into practice in the workplace. Their experiences offer hope for leaders and organizations at various stages of the DE&I journey, and can be summarized by the following pieces of advice:

- Visible CEO commitment, leadership, support, and cover are critical.
- An infrastructure must be in place that includes dedicated resources, data collection software, and shared accountability.
- Intentionally embed DE&I into all functions of the organization.
- Create SMART (specific, measurable, achievable/action oriented, realistic/relevant, and time-bound) goals.
- Use data and metrics to inform decision making, strategy, programs, and policies.
- Remember that process and policy lead to sustainability.
- Disrupt systems that perpetuate inequities.
- Be curious and seek out learning opportunities.
- Network with other DE&I practitioners, including those who don't look like you.
- Don't quit. Implement, test, pause, reflect, iterate, reroute but keep moving forward.

Thank You to Our Contributors

This guide would not have been possible without the insights of many exemplary West Michigan workforce diversity, equity, and inclusion officers. In addition to being leaders in this field, the contributors represent various dimensions of diversity, including age, gender, sexual orientation, race, ethnicity, education level, socioeconomic status and geographic location. They shared personal and professional experiences, challenges, knowledge, and unique perspectives. Their contributions, to our community as well as this guide, are greatly appreciated.

Robyn Afrik
Director of Diversity, Equity and Inclusion, Ottawa County

Jesse M. Bernal, Ph.D.
Vice President for Inclusion and Equity & Executive Associate for Presidential Initiatives, Grand Valley State University

Rhae-Ann Booker, Ph.D.
Vice President of Diversity, Equity & Inclusion, University of Michigan Health-West

Latoya Booker
Executive Director of Diversity Equity and Inclusion, Davenport University

Abe Carrillo
Associate Vice President, Global Inclusion & Diversity, HDR Inc.

B. Afeni McNeely Cobham, Ph.D.
Chief Equity and Inclusion Officer, Grand Rapids Community College

Kenneth James
Chief Diversity Officer, Muskegon Community College
(Formerly Director of Inclusion, Grand Rapids Area Chamber of Commerce)

Jackie Lillie
Director, Americas Inclusiveness Office, EY

Michelle R. Loyd-Paige, Ph.D.
Executive Associate to the President for Diversity & Inclusion, Calvin University

Joe Matthews
Vice President of Diversity, Equity & Inclusion, Gentex Corporation

Candy S. McCorkle, Ph.D.
Vice President of Diversity and Inclusion, Western Michigan University

Brandy Lovelady Mitchell, Ed.D.
Director of Diversity, Equity and Inclusion, Michigan Education Association

(Formerly Director of Diversity, Equity, and Inclusion for Kent Intermediate School District)

Ann Noe
Inclusiveness & Diversity Senior Program Manager, Herman Miller

Darius Quinn
Human Resources Manager and DEI Leader, Kent County

Courtney Simmons
Equity and Inclusion Director, Bell's Brewery, LLC.

(Formerly Inclusiveness & Diversity Senior Program Manager, Herman Miller)

Additional Thanks

- Bill Guest, President and Chief Solutions Architect, Metrics Reporting, Inc., and John Cleveland, President, Innovation Network Communities, for valuable guidance and thought leadership to the development of this guide.

- Talent 2025, a key project partner that has been working with business leaders since 2014 through their Diversity and Inclusion Working Group to help attract, develop, and retain more diverse talent in West Michigan.

- The Doug and Maria DeVos Foundation, which provided key funding for this project as part of TalNet, the Talent Innovation Network of West Michigan.

Methodology

- Research started with a national scan of leading practices.

- A series of human-centered design interviews were held with 15 DE&I leaders who serve internal to their organizations.

- Insights collected from the interviews were organized into themes, which later became the top five competencies outlined in this guide.

- Additional content was transformed into competency statements and practical workforce application examples.

- The aggregate data collected from research and interviews was organized into a draft guide.

- The draft guide was reviewed by the 15 contributors and additional DE&I practitioners in a series of focus groups.

- This is the second edition of this publication. The first edition was titled *Diversity and Inclusion: Five Essential Leadership Competencies of an Effective D&I Practitioner.* The content will be reviewed and refined as needed in future editions.

About Talent 2025

Talent 2025 is a catalyst working to ensure an ongoing supply of world-class talent for West Michigan. Composed of over 100 CEOs from the region, Talent 2025 illuminates gaps, evaluates leading practices, and advocates for the implementation of those leading practices to make West Michigan a top 20 employment region by the year 2025.

Talent 2025 serves 13 counties in West Michigan, embracing the industries, businesses, and educational institutions of each county. The organization convenes stakeholders from each of these sectors and facilitates an efficient collaboration that integrates resources, streamlines processes, and leverages energies to address the talent demand needs of each sector.

⊙TALENT 2025

Learn more at www.Talent2025.org

About TalNet

TalNet is a network of talent system innovators united in a commitment to accelerate economic mobility in West Michigan by improving the quality of career decisions in education, training, and job selection.

The goal of TalNet is to empower people to work in jobs where they are highly engaged, high performing, and earning good rewards.

TalNet supports this work by aligning the talent needs and hiring decisions of employers with the lifelong career journeys of students and job seekers.

Learn more at www.TalNet.org

About the Author

Whitney White is a certified facilitator for Implicit Bias and Cultural Intelligence, and a Certified Diversity and Inclusion Recruiter. She has completed diversity, equity, and inclusion trainings on leadership, inclusive workplace culture, belonging, healing racism, cultural competency, and emotional intelligence.

Since 2016, Whitney has worked for Talent 2025 and currently serves as the Director of Employer Engagement. In this role, she works directly with CEOs, Human Resource Leaders, and Diversity Officers from more than 100 companies in West Michigan to lead regional diversity initiatives as well as support talent attraction, retention, and development efforts.

She earned a Bachelor of Science degree in Criminal Justice from Grand Valley State University and has completed graduate-level courses in Public Administration, Human Resources, and Public Policy. Her professional experience in Workforce Development ranges from helping job seekers overcome barriers to building trusted partnerships with human resource leaders to provide a portfolio of services to help them meet their talent needs.

Organization of the Guide

PAGE

Part 1: Why, What & How   1

Lays the foundation for the subsequent sections, starting with why West Michigan employers need support in their efforts to strengthen diversity, equity, and inclusion strategies, followed by what the guide provides and how those supports can be used. This section also includes frequently used terms and concludes with a summary of insights from West Michigan DE&I practitioners.

The Why: Addressing a Need	2
The What: Providing Guidance	3
The How: Using This Guide	4
Frequently Used Terms	5
The Perspective from West Michigan	7

PAGE

Part 2: Establishing a Solid Foundation   11

Examines the challenge of leading DE&I change. Although this guidebook focuses on competencies needed by DE&I officers, it is important to recognize the roles of top leadership, organizational culture, and infrastructure to support the work. This includes understanding that, for many, DE&I is a continuous journey toward the objective of equity.

The Tone from the Top	12
The Challenge of Leading DE&I Change	13
CEO Responsibilities	14
An Infrastructure for Success	16
Equity as a Destination	17
DE&I Impact Model	20

PAGE
Part 3: Individual Competencies 23

Provides a deeper dive into each of the five competencies. Each competency section begins with a quote and definition. These are followed by three to five competency statements, with examples of how the competency is applicable in the workplace. Supplementary context is also provided.

Five Key Competencies of a DE&I Leader	24
Competency Chapters	
Personal Characteristics	25
Knowledge	31
Planning	39
Leading	49
Communication	53

PAGE
Part 4: Improving Skills 57

Provides a self-assessment, reflection questions, and an action plan to improve DE&I leadership competencies.

Self-Assessment	58
Reflection	62
Action Plan	63

Conclusion

West Michigan Innovations	64

Appendix

References and Resources	67

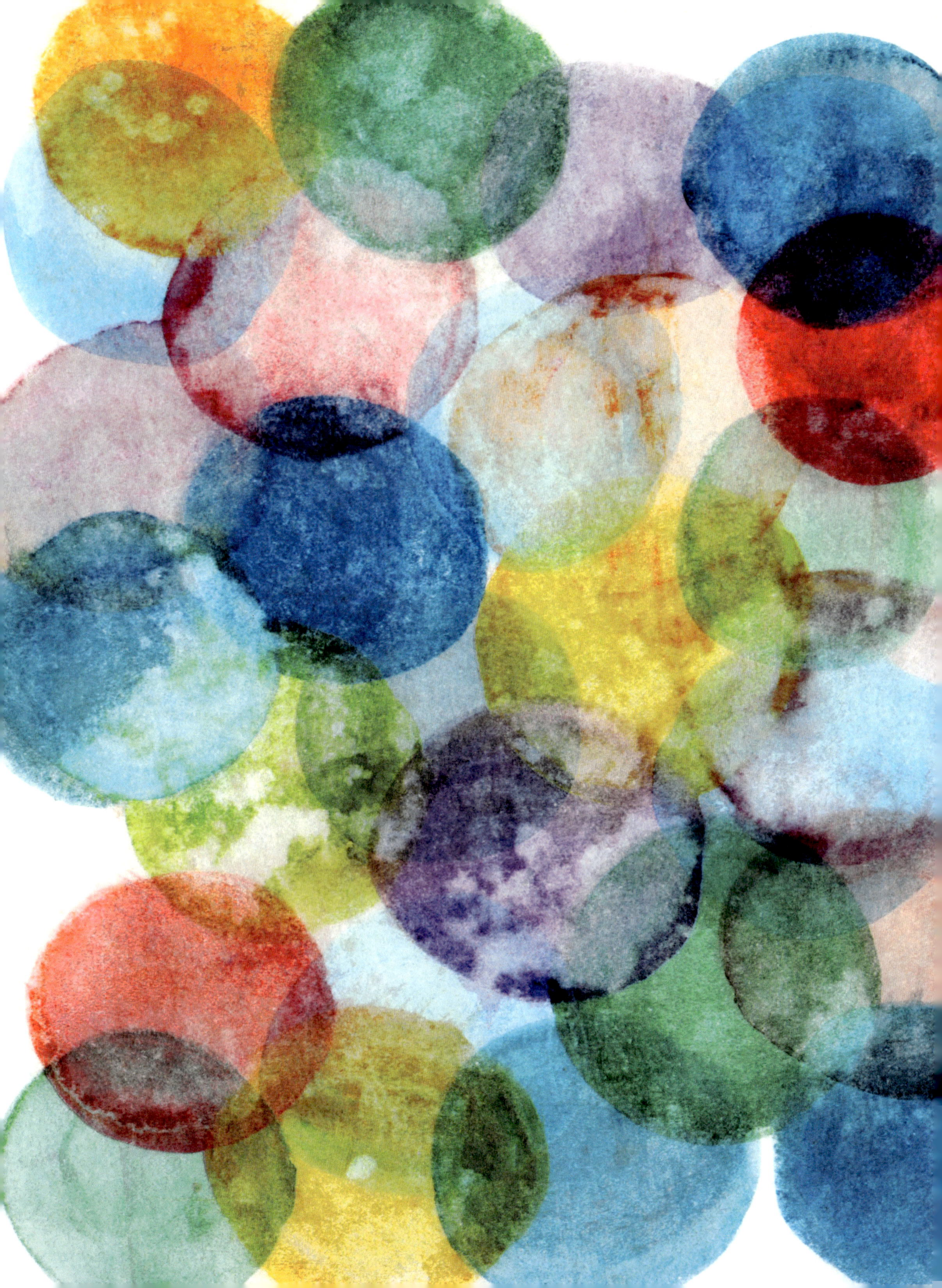

Part 1:

WHY WHAT & HOW

Laying the foundation for subsequent sections: Why West Michigan employers need support to strengthen diversity, equity, and inclusion, what the guide provides and how those supports can be used.

The Why: Addressing the Need

West Michigan employers are increasingly recognizing the importance of diversifying their workforces and creating an environment of inclusion and belonging. There is a growing understanding of how diversity, equity, and inclusion help companies meet talent needs, understand evolving consumer bases, and establish new markets.

Acknowledging the value of diversity, equity, and inclusion is a start. Companies across our region have demonstrated they also are ready to move beyond statements by taking action to embark on a journey that leads to impact.

Even as more companies create diversity officer positions or delegate this important responsibility to human resource leaders, they often lack guidance on how to set the DE&I officer up for success through selecting the best candidate, developing an infrastructure that supports change, and promoting continued professional development. Specific competencies are required to facilitate DE&I efforts across an organization.

The business case for diversity, equity, and inclusion is well-researched and documented. Numerous studies have shown the positive correlations between a diverse workforce and an organization's overall performance. However, similar documentation is scarce for the key competencies, roles, and responsibilities needed to deliver these positive outcomes. Many DE&I leaders are appointed to that role without receiving any formal training or a game plan.

This guide is designed to fill these gaps.

The What: Providing Guidance

The guide is intended as a resource to support the professional development of DE&I officers, by identifying and defining the top five competencies needed to be effective.

Building on existing national research and leveraging the insights of leading West Michigan DE&I practitioners, the guide outlines essential roles and responsibilities. It highlights what leaders need to know and be able to do.

At the same time, the guide seeks to help advance DE&I as a field of practice in West Michigan.

DE&I is relatively new when compared to more established fields, such as medicine, manufacturing, or industrial psychology. Diversity training itself did not become widespread in corporate America until the 1980s and even then, the motivation was primarily to protect against civil rights lawsuits. (Vaughn, 2007, pp. 11-16) While DE&I certification programs are becoming more prevalent, few bachelor's or master's level degree programs exist. Many colleges and universities offer classes on these topics under degrees in organizational development, leadership, or interdisciplinary studies.

According to Innovation Network for Communities (INC), "Fields evolve in stages. Fields have some common elements, and the work on each element changes over time. Healthy fields create the 'ecology' out of which many innovations emerge. Clusters of innovation are the core of field development."

Applying the INC Evolution of Practice Fields framework below, West Michigan organizations appear to be at Stage 1 (framing) and Stage 2 (networking). This guide seeks to help the region advance to stages 3 (maturation) and 4 (standardization).

The Evolution of Practice Fields: Four Stages

1 Framing	2 Networking	3 Maturation	4 Standardization
Conceptual framing and isolated practice examples.	Networking of innovators and the proliferation of practices. Practices are fragmented and often considered "proprietary."	Maturation of practices; convergence around common methods and tools; integration of previously differentiated practices; development of a professional implementation support network.	Practices become highly standardized and incorporated into formal systems for training, credentialing, and certification. Practices are considered "commodities." Reward systems reinforce desired behaviors.

Current state of West Michigan, Dec. 2021

Source: Field Building, 2007, by Innovation Network for Communities. www.in4c.net

The How: Using the Guide

- As companies create DE&I officer positions, the guide can be a resource to develop job descriptions and support hiring to fill that role.

- This guide can be used as a training supplement to support the onboarding of new DE&I officers.

- Experienced practitioners can use the guide as a reference source for leading practices that drive positive outcomes.

- This guide can be used to support the West Michigan community, by articulating a clear and consistent set of competencies needed to lead DE&I.

- This guide provides examples of resources that can be used to elevate skills related to specific competencies. The examples are not intended to be an exhaustive list, but merely a starting point.

- The guide is not designed to replace any organization's current DE&I structures.

- Note also that every DE&I officer should remain aware of the implications of state and federal laws. Employers with government contracts need to work with their legal teams to ensure compliance with the latest regulations governing such topics as diversity, equity, and inclusion training.

- Before adopting any of the recommendations in this book, you are encouraged to consult with your chief diversity officer or other relevant leaders responsible for DE&I.

- The authors, contributors, and funders of this guide are not responsible for any liability, risk, or loss incurred as a result of any information presented.

Defining 'DE&I Officer'

The phrase "DE&I officer" is meant to describe any organizational leader responsible for internal diversity, equity, and inclusion efforts. DE&I officer roles and responsibilities vary greatly based on several factors, such as organization size, industry sector, leadership structure, company culture, vision, mission, and values. This guide focuses on workforce inclusion, meaning inside of the workplace.

D&I vs DE&I

The importance of equity cannot be overstated (see Part 2) but unfortunately the term tends to be used too casually.

Many use the words diversity, equity, and inclusion interchangeably. Although equity is often included in job titles in health care, government, and education, the terminology is not universally adopted and, more importantly, the concept is not widely understood.

Some employers exclude *equity* because it is not a part of their vision, mission, or values. Others understand the reality of where they are on the DE&I continuum. Their people and culture may not be ready for the conversation. They may not have policies, practices, or systems in place to realistically measure, track or achieve equity. For others, excluding the word equity is a preference.

Evolving Language

DE&I language is continuously evolving to adapt to shifting cultural, political, social, and economic landscapes. In this work, there has been a significant increase in the use of words like accessibility, belonging, and justice. Examples include IDEA (Inclusion, Diversity, Equity, and Accessibility) and JEDI (Justice, Equity, Diversity, and Inclusion). Organizations may place the words in a different order or change the name of a role, department, or program for various reasons. Name changes generally occur during program revamps, for branding purposes, and in hopes of sounding more innovative. All these terms describe important aspects of the work and some are gaining traction. However, none has been adopted globally at this time.

Frequently Used Terms

As with any field, DE&I has its own technical language and jargon. Some terms may have multiple definitions depending on the context or source.

Some frequently used terms are detailed below. This is not an all-inclusive list; rather, it focuses on concepts examined and referenced in the following chapters.

Belonging
Ability to show up authentically and be accepted. A sense of being recognized as a valuable contributor, and member of the group. Genuinely feeling in solidarity with others. According to racial equity strategist and educator Dr. Darnisa Amante-Jackson, belonging is an ongoing culture created to have all people feel welcome across difference. It is manifested in relationships, conversations, physical space and written word.

Bias
A positive or negative inclination toward a person, group, or community; can lead to stereotyping.

Culture
A social system of meaning and custom that is developed by a group of people to assure its adaptation and survival. These groups are distinguished by a set of unspoken rules that shape values, beliefs, habits, patterns of thinking, behaviors, and styles of communication.

Cultural Competence
1) Knowledge, awareness, and interpersonal skills that allow individuals to increase their understanding, sensitivity, appreciation, and responsiveness to cultural differences and the interactions resulting from them. The particulars of acquiring cultural competency vary among different groups, and they involve ongoing relational processes tending to inclusion and trust building.
2) A process of learning that leads to the ability to effectively respond to the challenges and opportunities posed by the presence of social and cultural diversity in a defined social system.

Cultural Intelligence (CQ)
A capability to work effectively across national, ethnic, and organizational cultures. Evidence-based strategies exist to help individuals and organizations enhance their CQ skills. (SHRM, Cultural Intelligence, 1)

Diversity
Psychological, physical, and social differences that occur among any and all individuals; including but not limited to race, ethnicity, nationality, socioeconomic status, religion, education, marital status, language, age, gender, sexual orientation, mental or physical ability, viewpoints, and learning styles. A diverse group, community, or organization is one in which a variety of social and cultural characteristics exist.

Equality
Evenly distributed access to resources and opportunity necessary for a safe and healthy life; uniform distribution of access to ensure fairness.

Equity
The guarantee of fair treatment, access, opportunity, and advancement combined with an effort to identify and eliminate barriers that have prevented the full participation of some groups.

The principle of equity acknowledges that there are historically underserved and underrepresented populations and that fairness regarding these unbalanced conditions is needed to assist equality in the provision of effective opportunities to all groups.

Note that equity is an important and complex topic addressed at greater length in Part 2.

Fairness
Treating others equitably, regardless of your personal preferences, biases, or beliefs. Includes making sure that opportunities for development and advancement are distributed evenly and being aware of how your biases intersect with the choices and decisions you make.

Source: (Equity: How to design organizations where everyone thrives, 2021, by Minal Bopaiah.)

Inclusion
The act of creating environments in which any individual or group can be and feel welcomed, respected, supported, and valued to fully participate. An inclusive and welcoming climate embraces differences and offers respect in words and actions for all people.

Intersectionality
The ways in which oppressive institutions (racism, sexism, homophobia, transphobia, ableism, xenophobia, classism, etc.) are interconnected and cannot be examined separately from one another.

Marginalization
The placement of minority groups and cultures outside mainstream society. All that varies from the norm of the dominant culture is devalued and at times perceived as deviant and regressive.

Cautions About Terminology

Diversity as a Proxy for "Underrepresented" or "Black and Brown"
Organizational diversity encompasses all of its members — including majority group members. By being intentional about understanding which identities are underrepresented, it is possible to increase representation by adding additional diversity. This does not mean seeking "diverse individuals." It means seeking individuals with a broad range of experiences that may be missing from organizations.

Person-First or Identity-First Language
Opinions on using person-first or identity-first language vary within the disability community. Person-first language attempts to describe a person as more than their disability by placing emphasis on the person ahead of the disability. Examples would be "a person with autism" or "a person who is blind." Identity-first language is preferred by individuals who view their disability as a permanent and inextricable part of who they are. Examples of this would be saying "an autistic person" or "a blind person." As with the other aspects of identity that have been addressed in this guidebook, it is important to ask an individual how they like to be described and addressed. There is no one-size-fits-all.

Minority
While the intent is to communicate a person is from a group smaller in number, the reality is that our global demographics reflect that we have a "minority majority" as people-of-color populations grow beyond white populations. Not only is the term "minority" becoming a false notion, but the unintended impact is that it often is considered a pejorative. While one's group representation might be small, it doesn't make their person small nor their contribution any less significant. In fact, with "culture add" in mind, an underrepresented perspective becomes even more important to the organization.

Other inclusive language terms can be found here: https://seeds.sproutsocial.com/writing/inclusive-language/

Readers interested in an extended glossary may want to review the Diversity Best Practices Research Report, "Glossary of Terms for Diversity, Equity, and Inclusion," cited in the Appendix. Unless otherwise cited, the preceding definitions are drawn from that report.

The Perspective from West Michigan

In the human-centered design interviews used to inform this guide, DE&I officers were asked to analyze what it takes to succeed in their roles. Their insights appear throughout the guide, but several noteworthy themes emerged as keys to success for the individual as well as the organization.

Success Factors
- An officer must use data and research to guide strategy, consult various departments, review policies to reduce bias, track and analyze relevant metrics, and be able to influence various teams.
- DE&I officers must demonstrate commitment and unwavering values.
- Successful officers have foundational knowledge and the drive to continuously learn new content and develop their skills.
- Effective strategies are developed from research-based models or frameworks.
- The personal characteristics of the DE&I leader matter (i.e. approachable, vulnerable, empathetic).
- For organizations with 700 or more employees, it is recommended to have at least one full-time employee lead this work.
- People leave. Programs fail. Policy and process are what lead to scalability and sustainability.
- Resources (personnel and financial) must be dedicated to DE&I.
- The competencies considered most important can vary, based on:
  - the stage of the DE&I journey for the individual DE&I leader (professional, personal, educational, or motivational)
  - the DE&I officers' role (title, authority, and influence)
  - the stage of the DE&I journey for the organization
  - how success is defined by the organization
  - the systems that hold DE&I officers accountable
  - if a sustainability plan has been developed

What Does Not Work
Research consistently shows companies that excel at DE&I understand the following practices do not work:
- Appointing a person to lead DE&I solely because they are a person of color, member of an underrepresented group, or have displayed interest in the topic.
- Thinking that appointing a diversity officer is the silver bullet that will solve all your organization's people problems and inclusion challenges.
- Thinking DE&I programs are one-size-fits-all or that a "program" will solve all of an organization's diversity, equity, inclusion, or racism challenges.
- Adopting programs from other organizations without adapting to your specific company and industry needs.
- Expecting one underrepresented person to be the voice of the entire community (inside or outside the workplace).

> "The diversity officer should be respected and included as a key member of the executive leadership team."
>
> – JACKIE LILLIE, SPHR, SHRM-SCP,
> Director, Americas Inclusiveness Office, EY

"The way you help people connect to your DEI principles and framework can, and perhaps should, look different depending on your audience — but you should never compromise the content."

– LATOYA BOOKER
Executive Director of Diversity,
Equity & Inclusion, Davenport University

"Knowledge is important. Organizations have a tendency to assume that if you are a person of color, a person who identifies as non-binary, a person with a disability, etc., then you must be an expert on DE&I. That is not true. Just because a person is a member of a marginalized population, it doesn't mean that they will be the best at doing DE&I work."

— CANDY S. MCCORKLE, PH.D., Vice President of Diversity and Inclusion, Western Michigan University

Part 2: ESTABLISHING A SOLID FOUNDATION

Recognizing the roles of top leadership, organizational culture, and infrastructure to support work of DE&I officers. Understanding DE&I as a continuous journey toward the objective of equity.

The Tone from the Top

Although this guidebook is designed specifically to support the professional development of DE&I officers, it is important to acknowledge that this work does not take place in a vacuum. In fact, the most effective DE&I officer cannot succeed if certain organizational requirements are not in place.

These requirements are even more important within the current environment, when DE&I officers are being asked to solve problems that are systemic. CEOs must be committed to leading change efforts while setting the tone for top leadership and middle managers, which ultimately influences the organization's culture. CEOs need to understand a DE&I officer alone will not solve their problems with racism or other structural exclusions.

These commitments must go beyond verbal affirmations. DE&I officers must be supported with an infrastructure that allows this work to be implemented and sustained. Even those organizations not ready to embrace the concept of equity must acknowledge that DE&I is a perpetual journey, with equity as the ideal being pursued.

Leaders need to trust DE&I officers to offer alternative perspectives and to be the organization's subject matter experts. CEOs need to allow the DE&I officer to push and respectfully challenge.

This section will cover:
- The challenges of leading DE&I change
- CEO responsibilities
- An infrastructure for success
- Equity as a destination
- An overview of the DE&I Impact Model

> "There is a limit to an individual's capacity for the broad breadth of expectations that we have for DE&I work. To expect any one individual to have all competencies in all areas is an unreasonable expectation. Instead, the organization should collectively have knowledge, skills, and a strategy around DE&I competencies."
>
> – JESSE M. BERNAL, PH.D.
> Vice President for Inclusion and Equity &
> Executive Associate for Presidential Initiatives,
> Grand Valley State University

The Challenge of Leading DE&I Change

Successfully implementing an effective DE&I strategy differs from the typical change management process. As a complex, expansive field that touches on often-sensitive topics, DE&I presents many factors for organizational leaders to consider:

- The topic can make people uncomfortable and even defensive.
- DE&I work involves more self-reflection and self-awareness because the work may require changing attitudes, behaviors, and individual beliefs.
- The work is personal, relationship-based, and at times emotional.
- Understanding why DE&I is important involves both a business and moral case.
- Everyone deserves a voice. This requires engaging every individual in an organization from C-Suite executives to front-line employees.
- The work is never finished, which is why individuals and companies often state they are on a DE&I journey. While specific programs may have exact start and end dates, the organizational culture is always developing.
- DE&I has high risk aversion. Some organizations avoid DE&I because they are afraid to make mistakes.
- The DE&I field is constantly evolving with new terminology, training opportunities, certifications, events, and advocacy groups.

"Chief Diversity Officers ... are too often caricatured as saviors. ... Their positions and work serve as absolution from the actual work necessary to achieve diversity and inclusion. The CDO is not a savior and should not be put in the position to act like one. The responsibility to establish clear goals, targets, timetables, and processes should not only predate the development of a CDO position, it should be evenly distributed across university leadership and middle management." — (THOMAS, 2020, p. 173)

CEO Responsibilities

The success of the DE&I leader's efforts relies heavily on the CEO and executive team's leadership, as well as the infrastructure they establish. Both need to empower the DE&I officer to lead change and advance the work. Although an effective DE&I leader equips senior leadership to be voices for DE&I, ultimate power lies with the CEO, who must champion this work.

The following checklist is provided as a resource for CEOs, as well as a reference for DE&I officers to assess the environment in which they must operate.

CEO Checklist / DE&I Officer Assessment

✓ Assess Your Organization & Know Your "Why"
- Assess the current state of the organization from perspectives of mindset, culture, and data.
- Determine if the organization is ready to bring in more diversity or change. If it is not ready, determine what needs to change.
- Determine and document your "Why" from a business and moral perspective. Why is DE&I important to you and the organization you lead?

✓ Top-Down Leadership is Key
- Position DE&I as a business imperative driven by the CEO.
- Ensure the executive team and middle level management are also DE&I champions leading the efforts.
- Model the behavior you wish to see replicated in your organization.
- Offer "cover" and visible support to the DE&I officer when they face resistance.
- Approach DE&I with a growth mindset and believe your abilities can be developed through dedication and hard work.
- Be clear and transparent when communicating your DE&I commitment, goals, mission, initiatives, and policies.

✓ Shared Accountability
- DE&I is not the responsibility of any one person or department. It involves every person in the organization. Influencers are needed at every level.
- Understand and articulate to others that the success of DE&I programs, strategies, and change efforts don't solely fall on the DE&I officer.
- Create shared accountability and expectations for various leaders and departments throughout the organization.
- Understand that simply hiring a DE&I officer is not enough to solve your organization's "people problems" or change an entire organizational culture.

CEO Checklist / DE&I Officer Assessment

✓ **Position DE&I Efforts and Leadership for Success**
- Ensure the DE&I officer reports directly to the CEO and has access to and support from other C-Suite leaders.
- Allow the DE&I officer to lead and not just manage.
- Grant a DE&I officer access to work collaboratively with other leaders and departments to facilitate conversations and change.
- Understand DE&I efforts take time and persistence.
- Invest appropriate resources (financial, personnel, software, and other systems) to allow assessment, program development, and change.

✓ **Embed DE&I Into Your Organization**
- Embed DE&I into the organization's vision, mission, values, and strategic plan.
- Insert DE&I principles into organizational practices, processes, policies, and procedures.
- Help create a culture of inclusion, welcoming, and belonging by developing DE&I definitions and standards.
- Empower leaders to help create a psychologically and physically safe workplace that nurtures all employees and DE&I efforts.

"Most chief diversity officer positions are called chief because of the leading practices that suggest that it needs to be an executive position in order to have the cross-cutting influence and to serve as a catalyst for the structural work that is needed to truly transform the culture and the individuals of the system. So, when we bring in diversity officers, it's important to have fertile ground – meaning there needs to be conditions and mechanisms in place to not only support the diversity officer, but the work that is cross-cutting, and that is organizational work."

– BRANDY LOVELADY MITCHELL, PH.D., Director of Diversity, Equity, and Inclusion, Michigan Education Association

An Infrastructure for Success

Although DE&I is a relatively new field of practice in corporate America, higher education has been a leader in this area for years. One outcome of this focus in higher education has been the development of infrastructure models.

For example, in the 2019 report "Now is the Time: Developing a High Impact Diversity and Inclusion Infrastructure at the College of New Jersey," Damon A. Williams, Ph.D., offers three archetypes of Chief Diversity Officer vertical structure: Collaborative Officer Model, Unit-Based Model, and Portfolio Divisional Model.

Although these archetypes were designed for higher education, the key characteristics, strengths, and weaknesses can be applied to other industry sectors as well. The following matrix was adapted from Williams' models:

Archetypes	Key Characteristics	Strengths	Weaknesses
Collaborative Officer Model	Limited staff support. Requires high-ranking title, personal leadership and ability to leverage limited resources	• Maintains current organizational structure • Flexibility to redefine role • Dedicated advisory role • Symbolic, public commitment	• More symbolic than material commitment • Emphasizes thought leadership over initiatives • Limits ability to collaborate • Unequal footing with other senior roles
Unit-Based Model	Requires same leadership as Collaborative Officer Model but adds staff of support, programming and research professionals, and diversity officers	• Moderate integration with organizational structure • Dedicated advisory role • Symbolic, public commitment • Enhances capacity to engage in collaborative relationships • More structure for engaging in diversity issues as strategic priority	• Potential conflict with diversity and general units outside the diversity leader's portfolio • More cost-intensive than Collaborative Officer Model
Portfolio Divisional Model	Distinguished by collaboration and presence of several direct reporting units in a vertically integrated portfolio, creating a dedicated divisional infrastructure	• Dedicated advisory role • Enhanced capacity to create new diversity deliverables and engage in collaborative relationships • Ability to leverage current diversity infrastructure • Creates economies of scale • Sends powerful message about organization's diversity agenda • Most vertically structured and professional archetype	• Integrated into traditional structure, may generate organizational conflict • Potential dissonance with dedicated diversity units not in leader's portfolio • Most cost-intensive model • Alignment of diversity units in common portfolio may be perceived as "ghettoizing diversity"

Equity as a Destination

Equity remains the ideal toward which all inclusion efforts must strive. Equity is essential for success, for the individual as well as the organization.

However, embracing equity requires some soul-searching. Employers should not and cannot claim they are working in the equity space unless they fully comprehend the concept. They must have people and processes in place to demonstrate how they are analyzing and addressing it in the workplace. Even if equity has not yet been universally adopted by all employers, it should be part of the desired future state.

This begins by understanding what "equity" means. In addition to the brief definition in Part 1, the illustrations included here provide an example. The role of the employer must be to recognize barriers to equitable outcomes, and to find strategies to address them.

Source: Robert Wood Johnson Foundation

Equality = Sameness
Everyone gets the same thing.

Equity = Fairness
Everyone gets the same opportunity and is provided what is needed to ensure a fair outcome. Equity is required to reach equality.

Establishing a Solid Foundation | 17

Examples of Equity in the Workplace

Increasing equitable outcomes is the goal for many organizations who engage in DE&I work. Advancing equity requires intentional actions to remove individual, group, and systemic barriers and biases that impede opportunities. Equity extends beyond bridging the opportunity gap and providing each person with what is needed to ensure fairness. Equity includes providing accessibility to employment, products, services, and facilities, regardless of mental and/or physical ability, socio-economic class, education, culture, race, color, gender identity, sexual orientation, ethnicity, religion, viewpoint, or age. To accomplish this, organizations must identify and eliminate messages, attitudes, behaviors, and policies that produce and reinforce unfair outcomes. Following are some examples of how equity could look in the workplace:

Representation

- Demographic representation in the workforce – in all departments, teams, levels of leadership, and the governing board of directors
- Ensuring everyone is given a voice and the opportunity to contribute to team discussions
- Individuals representing various identities are actively involved in company decision-making processes
- Proactively working to ensure staff diversity in succession planning

Compensation & Development

- Paying a livable wage
- Fair job design, classification, and compensation across race and gender
- Compensating contributors for their time and knowledge when they are utilized in a way that allows your company to benefit financially
- Conducting a wage analysis, researching discrepancies, and adjusting accordingly
- Offering all employees access to mentorship, sponsorship, career paths, professional development, and other promotional opportunities
- Creating nontraditional opportunities and support, especially for historically underrepresented, underserved, and marginalized groups
- Every individual having the opportunity to attain their full potential

Process & Policy

- Fair communication, access, and treatment
- Providing contact information for accommodation requests and communicating accessibility resources for persons with disabilities
- Utilizing minority-owned and women-owned businesses for procuring a portion of company goods and services
- Assessing practices, policies, and processes and taking action to reduce bias in employee recruitment, selection, hiring, and promotion
- Identifying and effectively responding to differences in individual and group outcomes
- Conducting an equity audit using a comprehensive benchmarking tool that assesses DE&I hiring and promotion rates, policies for talent acquisition and performance evaluations, and organizational leadership practices
- Implementing practices to minimize algorithmic bias when using technology and artificial intelligence for recruitment and software applications
- Evaluating and redesigning systems that reinforce observable behaviors that contribute to fair treatment

Website Content, Visuals, & Communications

- Including a detailed description and alt-text on every web image
- Using captions/subtitles on videos
- Providing sufficient contrast in terms of colors used for text and background colors
- Using adequate font sizes
- Ensuring web links are both underlined and appear in a different color
- Creating and providing a transcript for videos and podcasts
- Reducing the use of jargon and academic language
- Spelling out acronyms
- Offering literature in more than one language
- Utilizing translation services for linguistic inclusion
- Making content accessible to other countries

Facilities

- Entryways, buildings, meeting spaces, conference rooms, furniture, and restrooms are all accessible to persons who use wheelchairs
- Signage provided in different languages, including Braille
- Restrooms, changing rooms, and athletic facilities accommodate and are welcoming to all gender identities
- Providing lactation rooms for nursing mothers
- Artwork is representative, inclusive, non-threatening, does not reinforce stereotypes, and is not intentionally offensive
- Color schemes and lighting are sufficient for individuals who are color blind or visually impaired

For more on equity, visit: https://theequitybook.com/equity-toolkit/

> "It's not just the influencing of CDO's (chief diversity officers). It's the ability to get folks to see themselves as part of this work. We alienate people by focusing on marginalized populations. In order for DE&I to be effective, you have to help those from the dominant group see themselves as part of it. 'How does this relate to me?' When you help the dominant group see that they are included, that's when you get them to invest."
>
> – CANDY S. MCCORKLE, PH.D,
> Vice President of Diversity and Inclusion,
> Western Michigan University

DE&I Impact Model

Many factors contribute to the successful integration of DE&I into corporate strategy, a company's overall improved performance, and equitable outcomes. The diagram below highlights the importance of people and process in leading to positive outcomes.

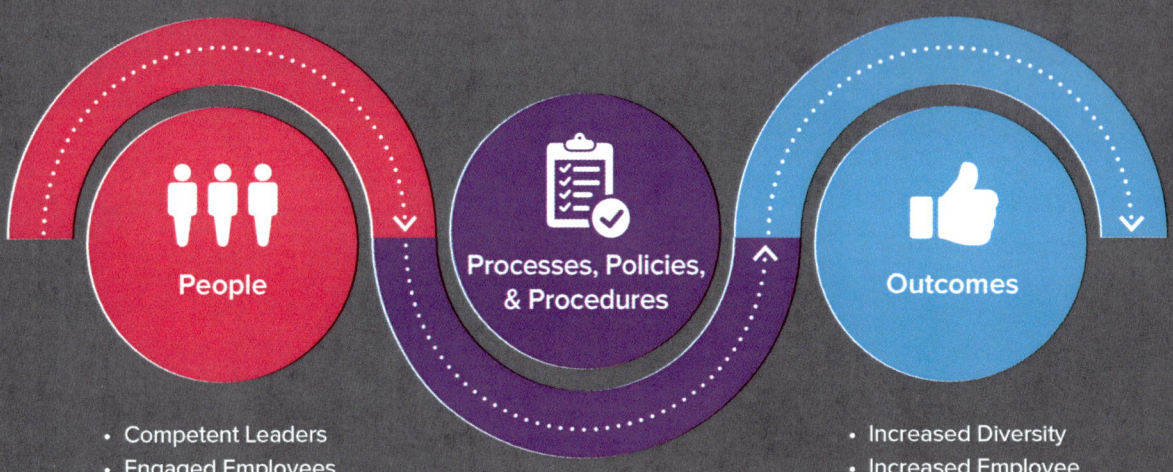

People
- Competent Leaders
- Engaged Employees
- Diverse Workforce
- Commitment to DE&I
- Growth Mindsets
- Foundational Knowledgebase
- Drive to Improve

Processes, Policies, & Procedures
- Talent Sourcing
- Talent Selection
- Benefits & Compensation
- Training & Development
- Talent Advancement
- Procurement
- Organizational Infrastructure
- Marketing & Branding
- Corporate Social Responsibility

Outcomes
- Increased Diversity
- Increased Employee Engagement
- Improved Collaboration
- Increased Innovation & Creativity
- Increased Productivity
- Increased Profitability
- Increased Inclusion & Belonging
- Improved Organizational Culture
- Equity

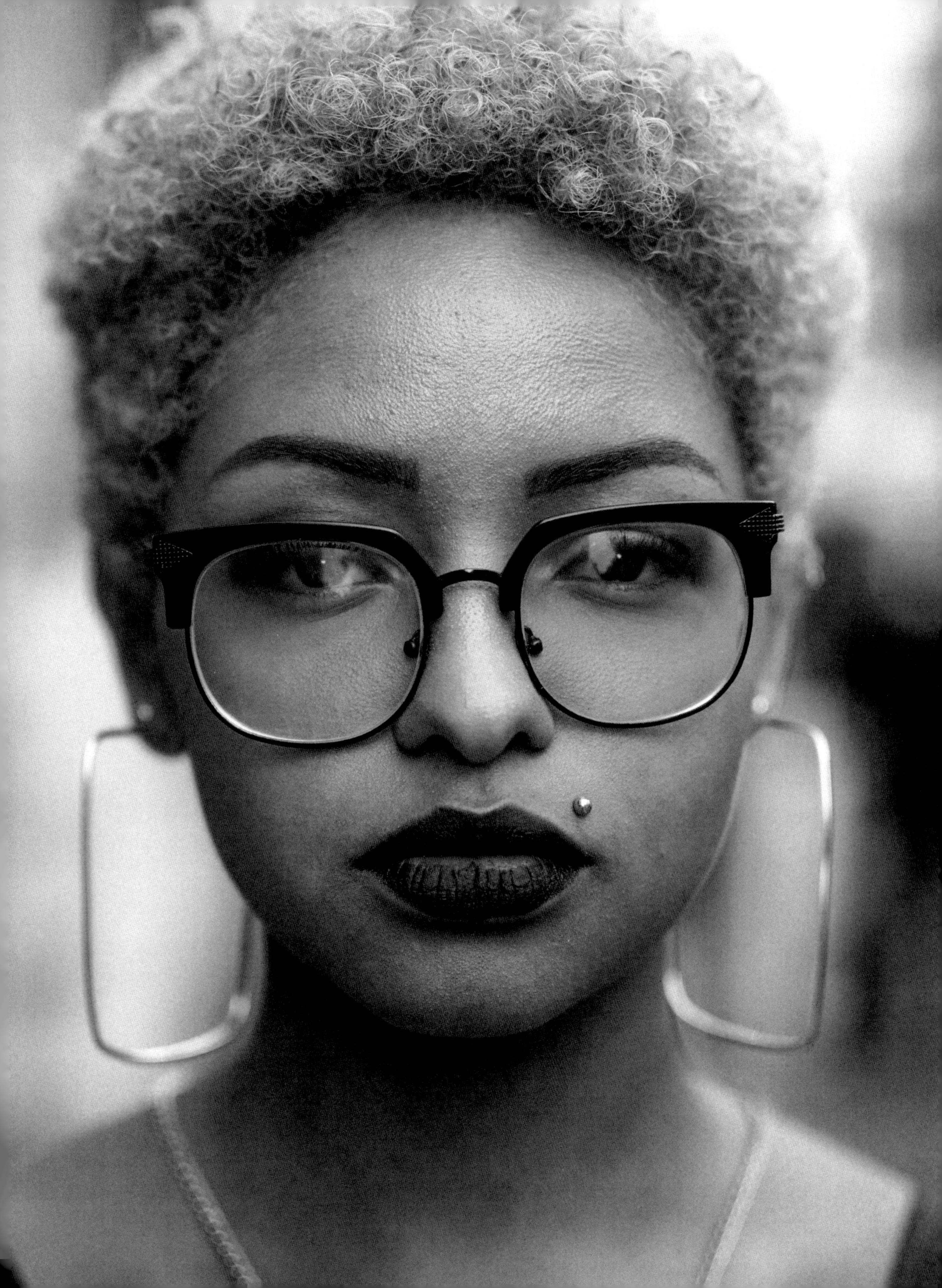

Part 3:
INDIVIDUAL COMPETENCIES

Diving deeper into each of the five competencies: Definitions, detailed competency statements, examples and context.

Five Key Competencies of a DE&I Leader

There are many important skills and attributes needed to be an effective DE&I officer. This guidebook will illuminate the top five identified by our research. The CEO should embrace and demonstrate these as well.

1 Personal Characteristics
Several factors that provide the ability to develop and foster meaningful relationships.

2 Knowledge
Having foundational understanding of DE&I and a commitment to continuous learning.

3 Planning
The ability to envision an ideal future state and develop a plan to achieve it.

4 Leading
The ability to influence people and systems to move organizations forward.

5 Communication
The ability to receive and share information in a number of formats.

In Part 3, each competency is examined individually in real-world contexts and applications, with resources for improvement. (Skill improvement will be covered in greater detail in Part 4 of the guide, where each of the competency statements will be revisited.)

Each of the following sections on Individual Competencies follows a similar format:
1. Competency definition with quotes from DE&I leaders.
2. Summary table of competency statements followed by workplace applications and examples.
3. Supporting resources to provide additional context and skill development.

Competency 1: Personal Characteristics

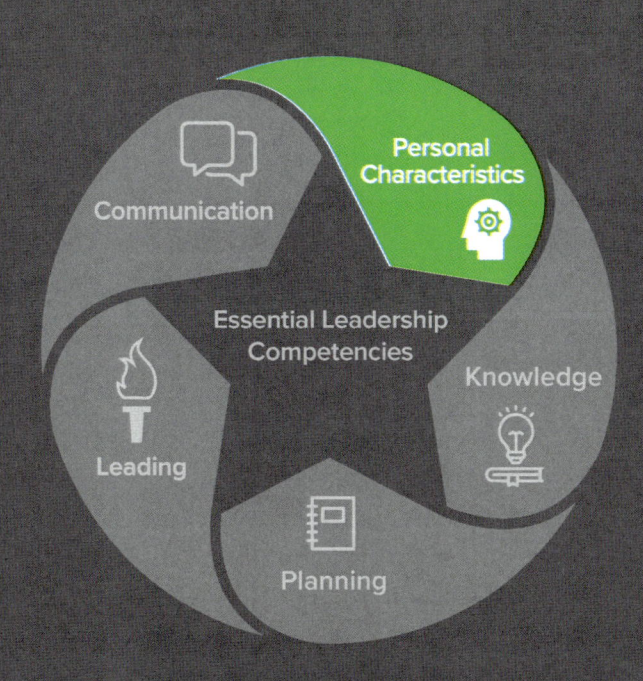

There are several individual attributes that increase the effectiveness of the DE&I officer. Those traits center around being authentic, curious, determined, and resilient while finding value in fostering meaningful relationships.

"Many approach DEI as a subject matter. It's a matter of not just the mind but the heart. A person needs a sincere desire to want to better understand others' experiences and to impact systems that fail to meet the needs of different groups."

– RHAE-ANN BOOKER, PH.D., Vice President of Diversity, Equity & Inclusion, University of Michigan Health-West

Personal Characteristics Competencies

In addition to being aware of their own cultural influences, effective DE&I leaders are resilient in the face of obstacles. They can distinguish what they really think and feel from what the situation actually requires. They are able to bracket their emotions and consistently choose to intentionally behave in a way that is acceptable in the workplace during uncomfortable encounters. They provide trustworthy leadership based on meaningful partnerships and are determined to accelerate change within their organizations.

Competency Statements

An effective DE&I officer should ...	Application
1 Be self-aware. Understand your own cultural influences, values, identities, triggers, dimensions of diversity and how you are situated within the organization, community, and world	• Understand your own privilege, cultural influences, identities, and the intersectionality of those identities • Acknowledge your own biases and "-isms" (additional information on isms can be found on page 33 and 36) • Maintain composure and self-control when interacting with others to cope with pressure, stress, criticism, and setbacks • Be self-directed • Operate with integrity • Determine if the goals and mission of the organization align with your personal goals, beliefs, and mission • Practice self-care to nourish your mental and physical health • Question your own assumptions and beliefs
2 Be resilient. Continuously move forward while encountering obstacles and lack of support	• Self-motivated – Initiative to undertake a task without another's supervision • Driver – Decisive, assertive and bold • Resolve – Determined • Courageous – Brave enough to lead difficult conversations, trainings and change management • Able to navigate ambiguity
3 Be authentic. Offer genuine and trustworthy leadership	• Humble – Seek perspectives that are different from your own; admit when you don't have the answer • Selectively vulnerable – Willing to share your own experiences • Open minded – Understand that all the answers do not come from a singular view • Understand the cost of authenticity in relation to social capital; authenticity may look different depending on the context
4 Be a catalyst. Spark or accelerate change within your organization	• Curious – Willing to ask questions about the organization's future goals and dedicated resources to achieve them • Innovative – Introduce new concepts, ways of thinking, and strategies • Passionate – Avid about understanding DE&I topics and advancing the work
5 Be relationship-oriented. Foster meaningful partnerships with colleagues and community stakeholders	• Collaborative – Willing to work with others to accomplish a shared goal • Approachable – Project a welcoming demeanor that is not intimidating • Connector – Link concepts to strategy and facilitate relationships between people when appropriate • Patient – Meet people where they are; it may take longer for some people to understand DE&I and become allies • Empathy – Show compassion • Flexible – Adaptable in approaches, problem solving, and innovation

The Importance of Humility

In 2014, the leading D&I think tank Catalyst conducted a global study to determine perceptions of inclusive leadership. The study of six countries revealed that one of the most significant indicators of an inclusive leader is humility, which they defined as "admitting mistakes, learning from criticism and different points of view, acknowledging and seeking contributions of others to overcome one's limitations." (Brown, 2019, p. 33.)

Personal Characteristics in Practice

Personality and character can be difficult to describe. When considered among all the dimensions of diversity *(see diagram in next section, Knowledge),* personality stands at the core of who we are as human beings. This has been the subject of study by philosophers and theologians for centuries. Only relatively recently has a psychological model emerged to gain wide acceptance. These "Big Five" traits, and how they apply to DE&I, are described further in the next section.

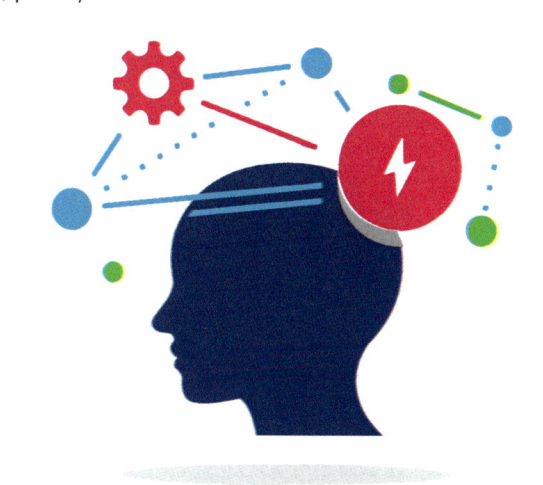

Most Useful Characteristics

Contributors to this guidebook were asked what personal characteristics are most useful for a diversity, equity, and inclusion officer. Here are some of their responses:

Robyn Afrik, *Director of Diversity, Equity and Inclusion, Ottawa County:*
"You've got to be resilient, determined, a driver and an influencer. There's also a level of intuitive discernment that's dialed into, all the time, because there's such a sophistication in the work that many do not (get to) see."

Michelle R. Loyd-Paige, Ph.D., *Executive Associate to the President for Diversity & Inclusion, Calvin University:*
"Self-awareness for the professional is the most important competency if you're going to be effective. This includes understanding your own identities, the intersection of your identities, and cultural awareness including the culture of your organization. Understanding what your personal triggers are and those of the organization. Self and organizational awareness are key in being able to move the needle. This is also important for conflict resolution for self and the organization."

Joe Matthews, *Vice President of Diversity, Equity & Inclusion, Gentex Corporation:*
"It takes a person to have some intestinal fortitude. In some cases, you are the only person in your company championing the effort. You have to be able to move forward knowing that people may be following you, but they are following you at a distance."

Ann Noe, *Inclusiveness & Diversity Sr. Program Manager, Herman Miller:*
"It's really important to be continually curious because with diversity work there is never a destination. You're always on a journey. You have to have a curious and growth mindset to do this work."

Examining Personality

Personality is the combination of characteristics or qualities that form an individual's distinctive character. We are each a unique combination of personality traits. *(Source: JOFI Personality Traits Worksheet)*

Despite their highly personal and variable nature, personality traits can be measured and used in hiring, including the selection of DE&I officers.

Multiple vendors offer assessments based on the "Big Five" model, consisting of Openness, Conscientiousness, Extraversion, Agreeableness and Emotional Stability.

Note that personality assessments are not meant to generalize individuals or groups of people, but to gain insights to build your cultural competence, enabling you to work more effectively across cultures. If you're using assessments, you still need to approach each relationship with a learner mindset.

The broadly accepted concept of the Big Five has roots in psychological research in the 1930s, further refined in the 1960s by American psychologist Lewis Goldberg. This psychological trait theory of the Big Five or the Five-Factor Model (FFM) was developed in the 1980s as a suggested taxonomy for grouping personality traits. (Ackerman, 2020)

Big Five Traits	What This Includes
Openness to Experience: *inventive/curious vs. consistent/cautious*	Appreciation for art, emotion, adventure, unusual ideas, curiosity, and variety of experience; reflects the degree of intellectual curiosity, creativity, and preference for novelty and variety a person has. Disagreement remains about how to interpret the openness factor, which is sometimes called "intellect" rather than openness to experience
Conscientious: *efficient/organized vs. easygoing/careless*	A tendency to show self-discipline, act dutifully, and aim for achievement; planned rather than spontaneous behavior; organized, and dependable
Extraversion: *outgoing/energetic vs. solitary/reserved*	Energy, positive emotions, surgency (cheerfulness and responsiveness), assertiveness, sociability, the tendency to seek stimulation in the company of others, and talkativeness
Agreeableness: *friendly/compassionate vs. analytical/detached*	A tendency to be compassionate and cooperative rather than suspicious and antagonistic toward others. This also is a measure of one's trusting and helpful nature, and whether a person is generally well-tempered or not
Emotional Stability: *secure/confident vs. sensitive/nervous*	The tendency to maintain poise and restraint to cope with pressure, stress, criticism, and setbacks. The opposite of emotional stability is neuroticism, the tendency to experience unpleasant emotions easily, such as anger, anxiety, depression, or vulnerability

Aligning the Big Five to DE&I

By establishing an understanding of the Big Five, it is possible to apply these concepts to those traits identified as important personal characteristic competencies for a diversity, equity, and inclusion officer:

- Curious
- Innovative
- Authentic

- Self-motivated
- Self-aware
- Discernment
- Resolve
- Determination

Openness
Conscientiousness
Emotional Stability
Extraversion
Agreeableness

- Resilient
- Vulnerable

- Passionate
- Driven
- Courageous

- Approachable
- Empathetic
- Humble
- Nurturing
- Patient
- Flexible
- Collaborative

Individual Competencies: Personal Characteristics | 29

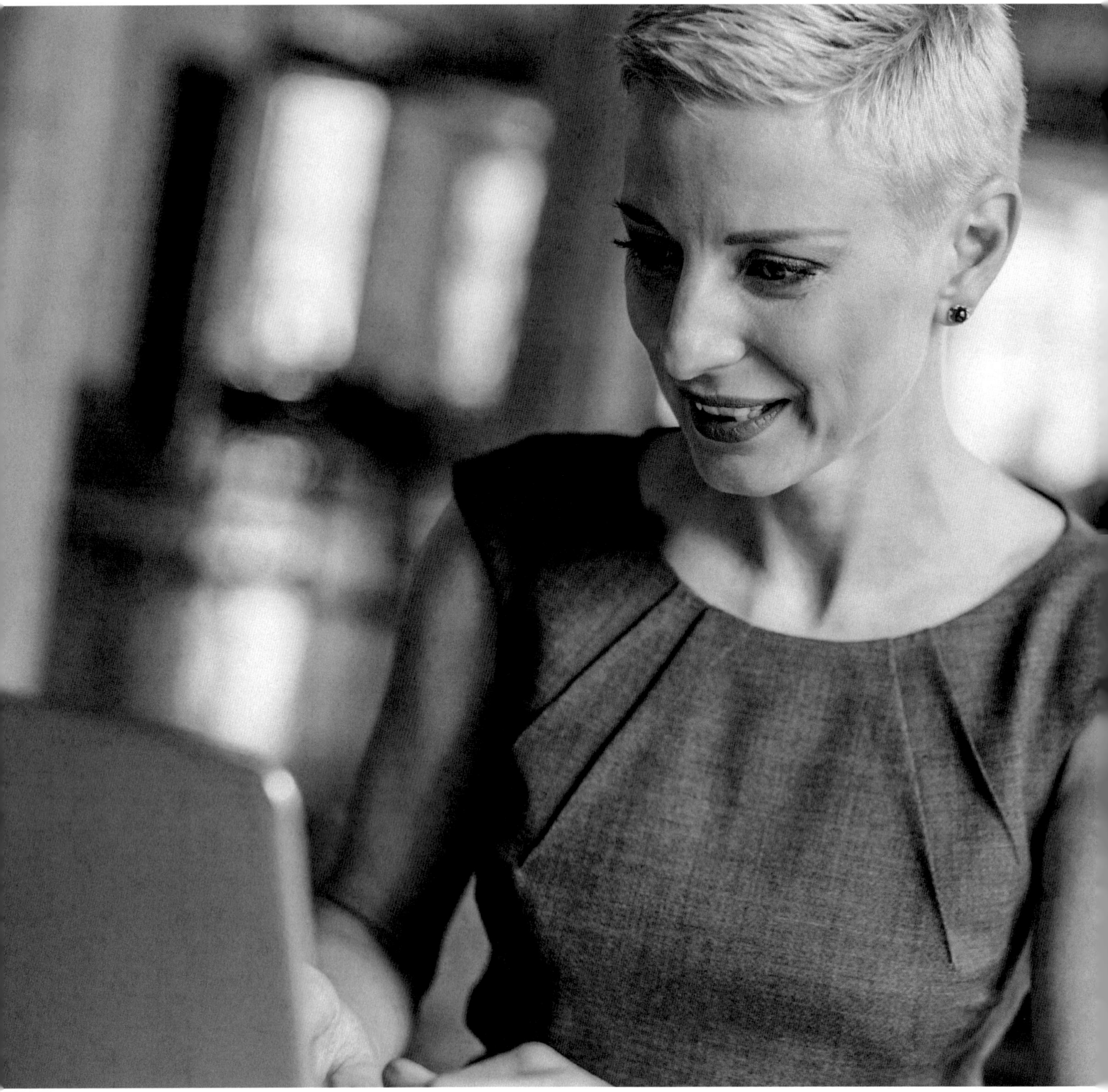

Competency 2: Knowledge

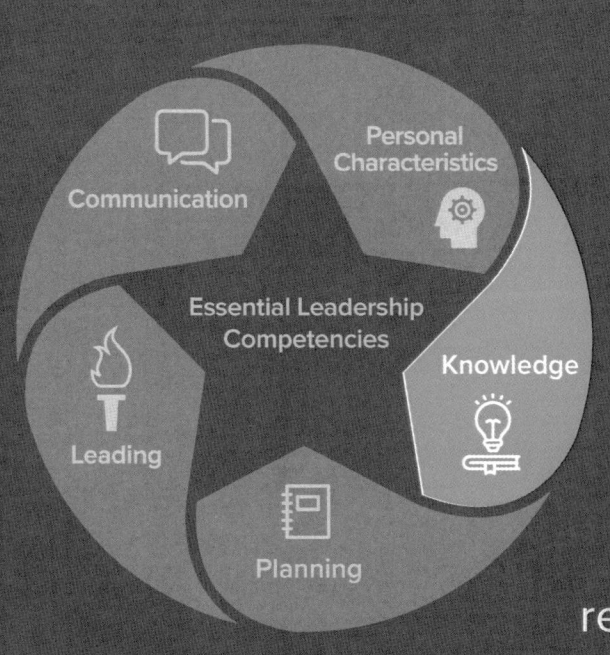

The role requires a foundational understanding of multiple diversity, equity, and inclusion topics. A willingness to engage in continued learning is essential as the DE&I field is constantly evolving with language, research, and practice. DE&I is a highly networked field. The collective impact of sharing knowledge and resources is more important than the competitive edge in this space.

"The Chief Diversity Officer must be a scholar-practitioner who can research, write, and speak about the intersectionality of socio-economic realities in the workforce."

– B. AFENI MCNEELY COBHAM, PH.D., Chief Equity and Inclusion Officer at Grand Rapids Community College

Knowledge Competencies

Starting with a strong foundation of knowledge in key content areas, an effective DE&I officer also engages in professional development, leverages insights from others, and researches best practices.

Competency Statements	
An effective DE&I officer should ...	**Application**
1 Develop content knowledge that is critical to effective DE&I strategies	• Understand the key content areas (bias; cultural competence; legal compliance; historical roots of racism and civil rights; systems of oppression; power and privilege dynamics; diversity hiring strategies; etc.). Additional topics to expand your knowledge base are on the next page • Engage in professional development (Continuing Education Units, conferences, informal learning, etc.) • Obtain relevant certifications
2 Create personal knowledge networks	• Leverage the insights and wisdoms of the various team members within your organization • Build trusted relationships with other DE&I leaders in your industry and region and beyond • Connect with other leaders who represent diversity dimensions that are different from your own • Seek out mentorship • Join leadership development groups and associations
3 Research DE&I standards and best practices, especially those that are relevant to your specific industry sector	• Attend relevant conferences and trainings on a local and national level • Study and apply national standards • Build cultural competence to better understand the differences between U.S. versus global operations

Expanding the Knowledge Base

It is impossible for one leader to be a subject matter expert or have experience in all DE&I areas. Instead, the organization should collectively build knowledge and a strategy around multiple DE&I topics.

The following topics can be explored in trainings for DE&I officers as well as be integrated into employee training programs or leadership meetings. The chart is not intended to be an exhaustive list, but merely a starting point. See the appendix for a list of certification programs, websites, and books to build capacity.

Topics for DE&I Officer Training

Foundational	Workplace	Race & Racism	Ism's*
• Allyship • Business case for DE&I • Communication • Cultural competency • Cultural intelligence • Cultural values • Diversity dimensions • Emotional intelligence • Holidays (federal, religious, and global) • Implicit bias / types of bias • Inclusive culture • Intent versus impact • Intersectionality • Microaggressions • Moral case for DE&I • Respect • Targeted universalism	• Belonging • Change management • Compassionate listening • Covering • Hostile work environments • Legal and compliance • Organizational culture • Othering • Power dynamics • Resistance to diversity • Talent recruitment and sourcing strategies • Unwritten rules and cultural norms	• Anti-racism • Aversive racism • Civil rights • Critical race theory • Individual racism • Institutional racism • Internalized racism • Interpersonal racism • Modern racism • Oppression • Privilege and identity • Structural racism • White fragility • White supremacy	• Ableism • Adultism • Ageism • Capitalism • Casteism • Cisgenderism/Homophobiasism/Transphobisms • Classism • Colonialism • Colorism • Cultural pluralism • Essentialism • Ethnocentrism • Eurocentrism • Feminism • Heterosexism • Lookism • Masculism • Multiculturalism • Pan-Africanism • Religious imperialism • Rugged individualism • Sexism • Sizeism

* "Isms" are a form of bias based on identities and/or beliefs held by individuals.

Foundational Understandings: Dimensions of Diversity

When discussing diversity and developing DE&I programs and strategies, it is important to remember there are many levels or dimensions of diversity. Many of these extend beyond visible physical attributes.

On a personal level, understanding the various dimensions will allow you to build and maintain more authentic relationships, which are especially important to keep moving forward when conflict or challenging situations arise. On a professional level, it will allow you to better leverage the differences of your workforce.

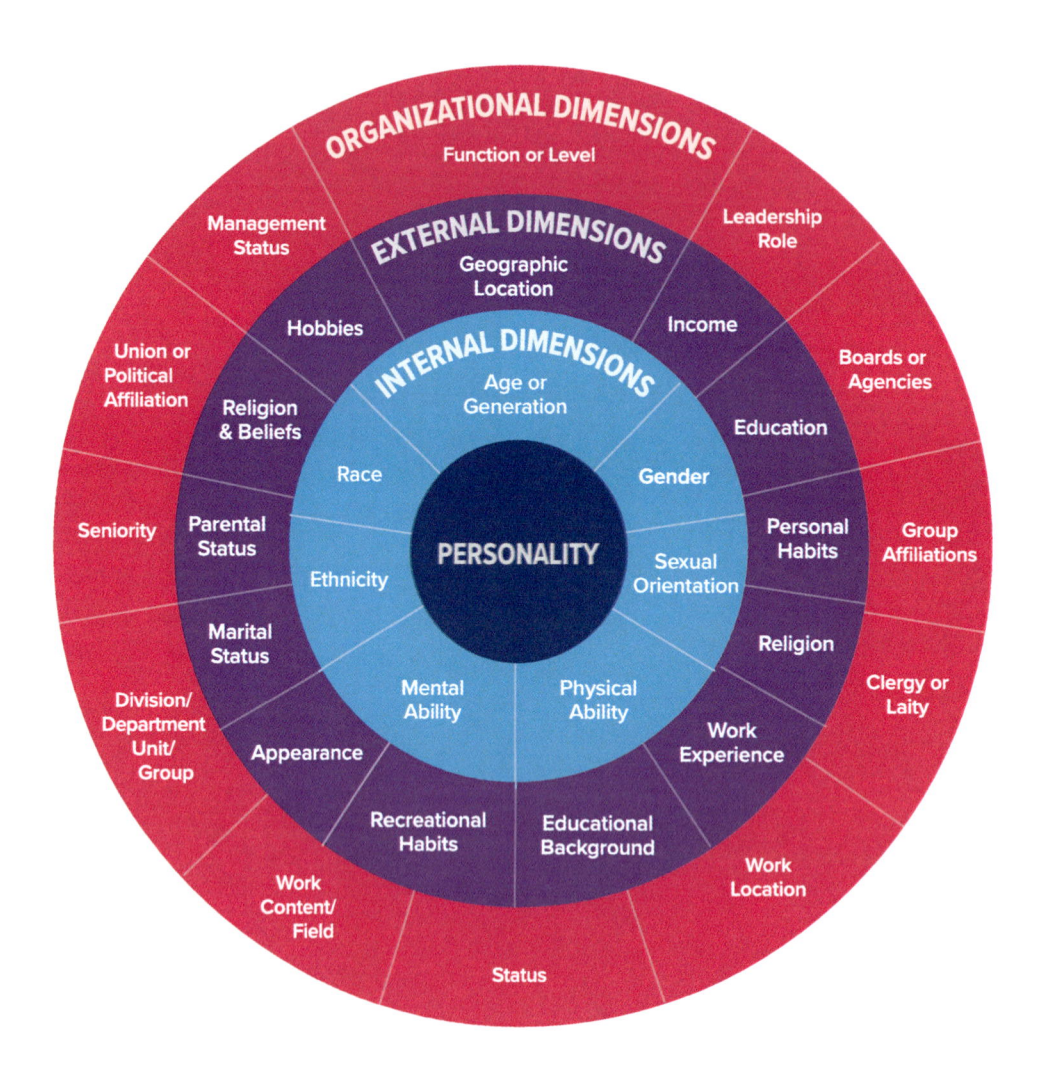

Diagram: Concentric circles showing dimensions of diversity.

PERSONALITY (center)

Internal Dimensions: Age or Generation, Gender, Sexual Orientation, Physical Ability, Mental Ability, Ethnicity, Race

External Dimensions: Geographic Location, Income, Education, Personal Habits, Religion, Work Experience, Educational Background, Recreational Habits, Appearance, Marital Status, Parental Status, Religion & Beliefs, Hobbies

Organizational Dimensions: Function or Level, Leadership Role, Boards or Agencies, Group Affiliations, Clergy or Laity, Work Location, Status, Work Content/Field, Division/Department Unit/Group, Seniority, Union or Political Affiliation, Management Status

> "If you're not leveraging your workforce and valuing that diversity, you're missing out on an opportunity. Everyone has to have a voice."
>
> – KENNETH JAMES, Chief Diversity Officer, Muskegon Community College

Another way of thinking about the dimensions of diversity is the metaphor of an iceberg, where there is much more than meets the eye. In this concept, the waterline represents the division between differences that can be seen and those that cannot.

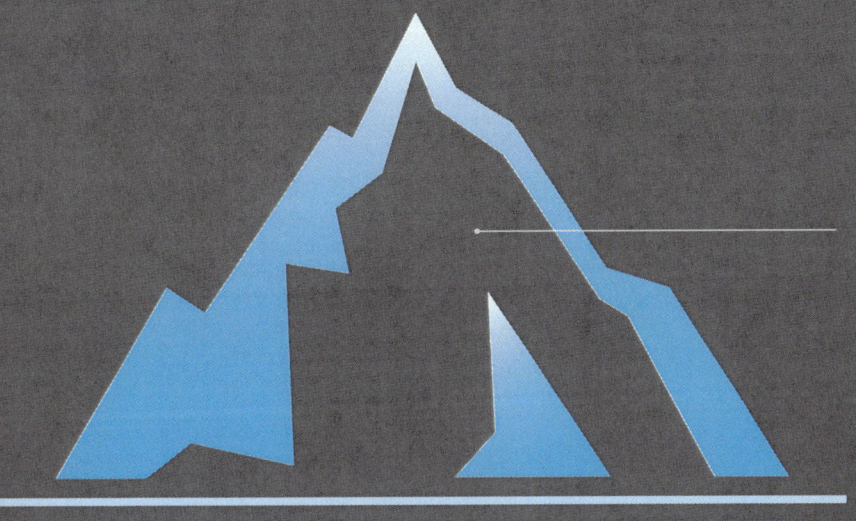

Tip of the Iceberg
Visual dimensions and characteristics that can lead to general assumptions, such as gender, skin color, race, ethnicity, physical attributes, and accent.

Waterline
Diversity dimensions such as ethnicity, physical ability, nationality, culture, languages spoken, and age that are implied after seeing or interacting with an individual.

Below the Waterline
Diversity dimensions that are not easily visible, such as values, beliefs, sexual orientation, religion, education, family status, life experience, work experience, military experience, culture, socio-economic status, marital status, parental status, native born/non-native, heritage, personality, work style, work role, function, political views, thinking style, and talents. Understanding this level of diversity requires asking questions and building authentic relationships with individuals.

Foundational Understandings: Types of Bias

Bias is defined as a prejudice in favor of or against one thing, person, group, or point of view compared with another, usually in a way considered to be unfair. "Unconscious" or "implicit" are the most common terms used to describe workplace bias. However, more than 30 types of cognitive bias can influence decision-making (Wood, 2015). Bias can appear in many forms and across all organizational levels, departments, and practices. Understanding the different types of bias makes it easier to recognize when they occur and to develop mitigation strategies.

Common Cognitive Biases

Affinity	Choice Supportive	Distance	Negativity	Recency Illusion
Anchoring	Clustering Illusion	Halo Effect	Normative	Salience
Attractiveness	Competence vs. Likeability	Horn Effect	Ostrich Effect	Selective Perception
Authority	Confirmation	In-group	Outcome	Self-enhancement (or overconfidence)
Availability Heuristic	Conformity	Information	Performance Attribution	Status Quo
Bandwagon Effect (Group Think)	Conservatism	Loss Aversion	Performance	Stereotyping
Benevolence	Correspondence	Liberalism	Placebo Effect	Survivorship
Blind-spot	Default Effect	Maternal	Pro Innovation	Zero-risk

"Bias reduces our ability to make decisions based on fairness, merit, and objectivity. ... Bias doesn't just affect the way we see others – it affects the way we view ourselves and our aptitude in supporting diversity and inclusion." – (Brown, 2019, p. 38)

Standards of Professional Practice in Higher Education

The competency statements listed on page 32 recommend researching DE&I standards and best practices that are relevant to your specific industry sector. In March of 2020, The National Association of Diversity Officers in Higher Education (NADOHE) published Standards of Professional Practice for Chief Diversity Officers in Higher Education 2.0. (Worthington, et al., 2020, pp. 1-22.) As implied, the standards they provide are heavily correlated to higher education and equity. However, some of the principles can be universally adopted, such as the ones below:

- Frame diversity, equity, and inclusion (DEI) work from comprehensive definitions that are inclusive and respect a wide range of identities
- Ensure DEI are embedded as imperatives in the institution's mission, values, and strategic plan
- Commit to plan, catalyze, facilitate, and evaluate processes
- Work with senior leaders to review and revise polices that create structural barriers for those who belong to marginalized and oppressed groups
- Work collaboratively to assess, plan, and develop infrastructure for DEI and institutional capacity
- Conduct climate assessments to illuminate strengths, challenges, and gaps in the development and advancement of DE&I
- Engage in a way that reflects the highest level of ethical practices

NADOHE holds a copyright for the Standards of Professional Practice, which is referenced with permission. Please see the appendix for a link to the full report.

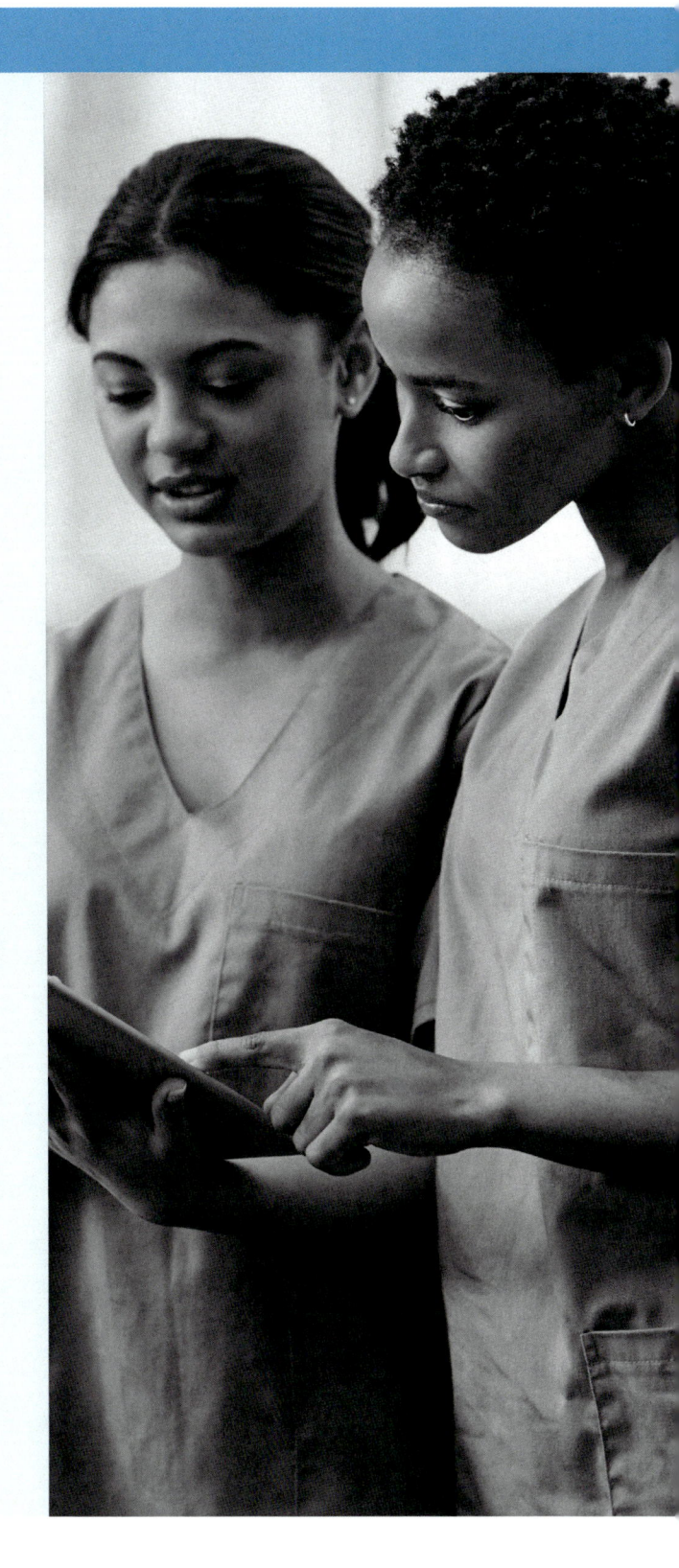

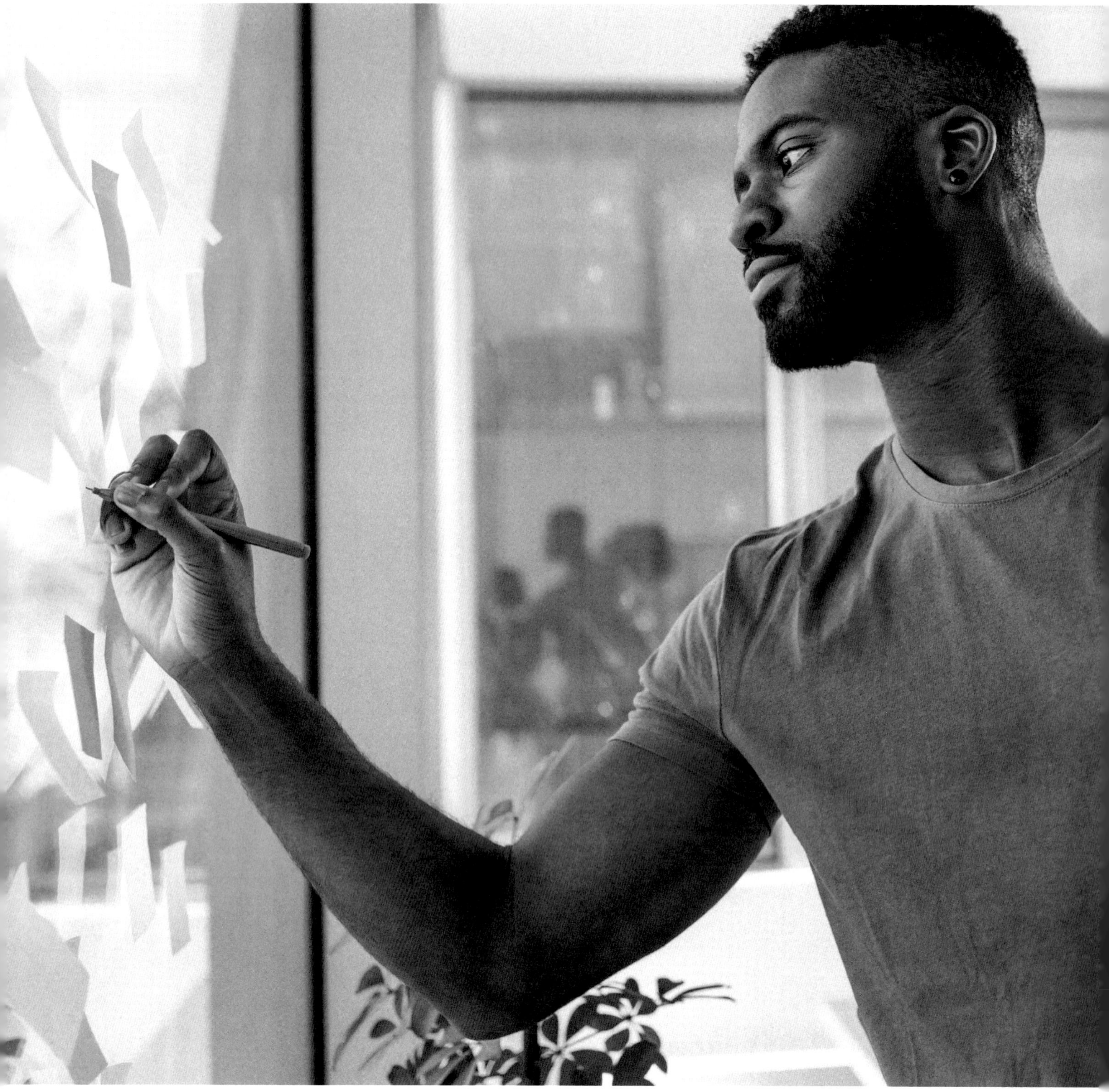

Competency 3:
Planning

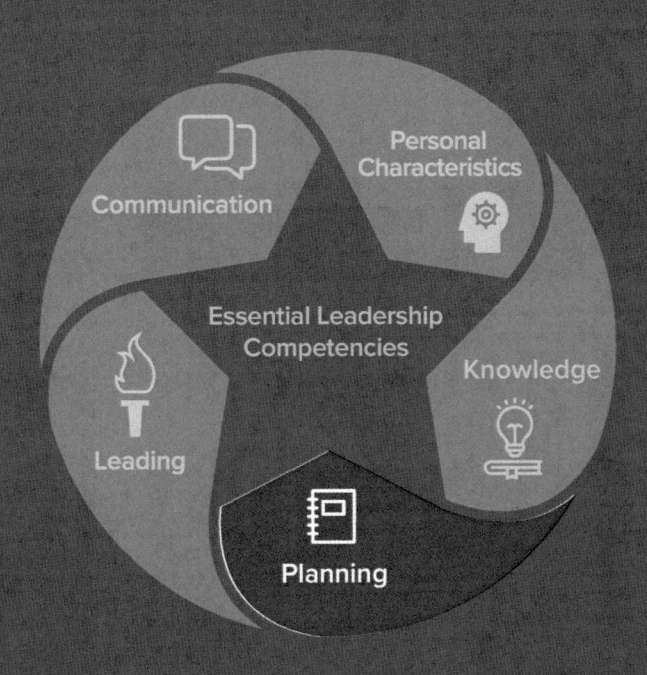

Strategic planning is a process, not a product. During this process, organizations envision their ideal future state and then develop specific plans, strategies, and actionable steps to achieve it.

"The thing to do with the future is not to forecast it, but to create it. The objectives of planning should be to design a desirable future and to invent ways to bring it about."

— RUSSELL ACKOFF, The Wharton School

Planning Competencies

Integrating a DE&I vision into an organization's overall strategic plan requires collaboration with and support from top leadership. Effective DE&I leaders should be able to define metrics and design, launch, and manage programs.

Competency Statements

An effective DE&I officer should …	Application
1 Use collaborative planning processes to integrate the organization's DE&I vision and tactics into the overall strategic plan	• Engage top leadership (executives and board of directors), middle-managers, individual contributers, and frontline staff • Understand the business deeply enough to connect DE&I efforts to core business success, including growth strategy, and sustainability • With the ideal future state in mind, create SMART (specific, measurable, achievable/action oriented, realistic/relevant, and time-bound) goals • Use cross-functional teams (human resources, organizational development, finance, procurement, marketing, data & metrics, affinity groups, etc.) • Hire external DE&I consultants and training providers as needed

2 Use data to assess the organization's current state and understand where the organization stands relative to its DE&I goals	• Advocate for the implementation of systems (processes, software, standardized definitions, etc.) to collect data
	• Define metrics that create shared accountability among various leaders and departments
	• Collect and analyze data to assess current state and evaluate performance on:
	  - Workforce demographics - Organizational culture
	  - Leadership mindsets - Inclusion index
	  - Employee satisfaction/engagement - Employee exit surveys
	  - Disaggregate data based on demographics and key intersections
	• Track the percentage of your total annual spend that is dedicated to purchasing from enterprises owned by minorities, women, veterans, people who have disabilities, and LGBTQ individuals
	• Display the data in a DE&I scorecard
	• Review data on a regular basis to track and measure progress and impact over time

3 Design, implement, and manage internal DE&I programs and initiatives (as needed)	• Develop employee recruiting and selection strategies that increase diverse representation • Establish and elevate opportunities to develop and retain employees, including mentorship, sponsorship, and career pathways • Beginning at onboarding, consistently deliver DE&I training to all employees to build capacity • Establish DE&I councils, employee resource groups, and/or affinity groups (when appropriate based on organization size and structure) • Challenge existing programs, practices and systems that are not demonstrating positive impact • Create a database of diverse vendors that align with your procurement needs (goods and services) • Create a formal supplier diversity plan
4 Create a shared DE&I culture across the organization	• Define common DE&I terms to create a shared language, with emphasis on terms like "culture fit" vs. "culture add" • Promote a sense of welcoming, inclusion, and belonging that provides psychological and physical safety to all employees • Review and adjust benefits and compensation packages to include nontraditional benefits such as flexible work schedules, and work from home options

The DE&I Continuum

Assessing and understanding the current state of your leaders and organization is essential to creating DE&I goals and planning. This process could begin by asking:

Is the organization ready to bring in more diversity? Is the organization ready to discuss and change the culture? If not, what needs to change?

Many companies find it helpful to rate themselves on a continuum. The example below is based on a model of the four stages of competence developed in the 1960s. A fifth stage has been added as a reminder that there is no end point in DE&I work. This is why these efforts often are referred to as a "DE&I journey."

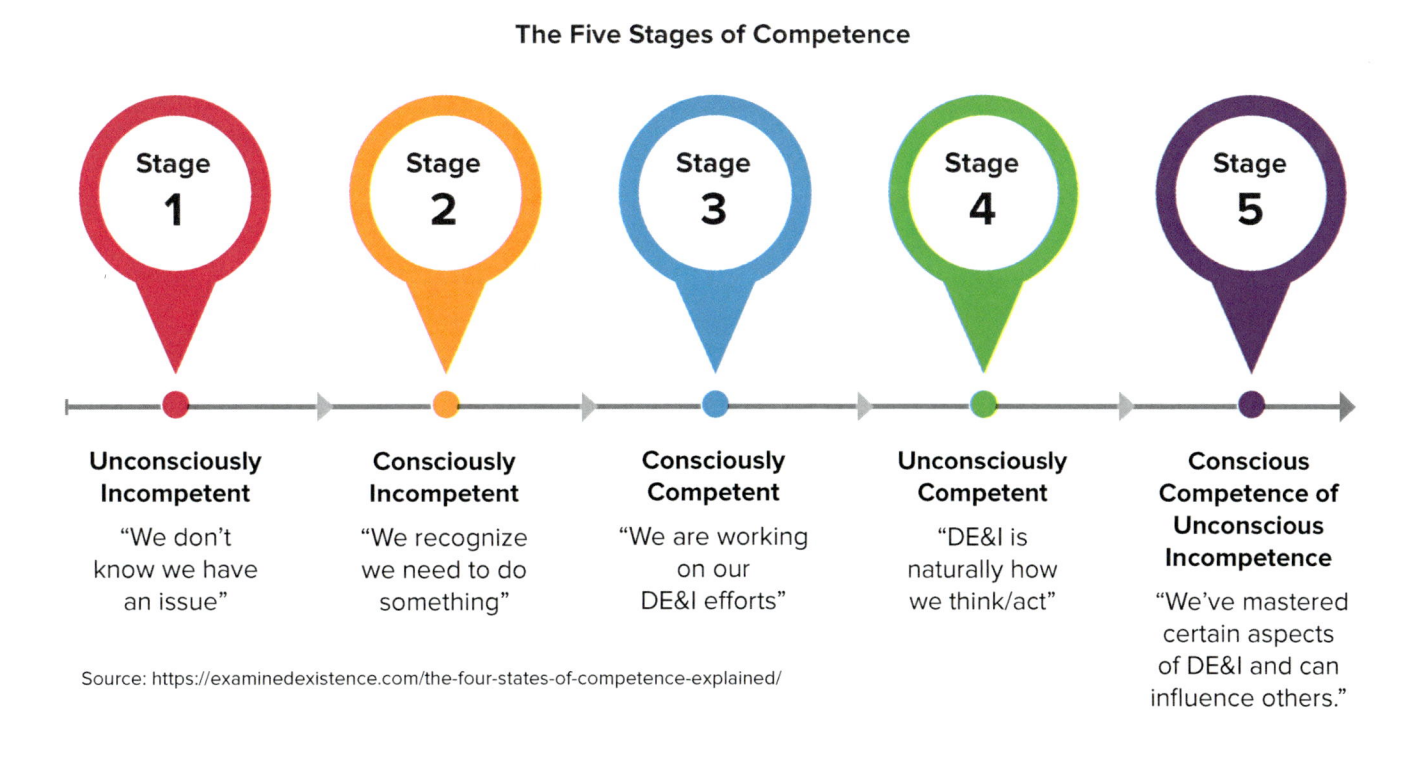

The Five Stages of Competence

Stage 1	Stage 2	Stage 3	Stage 4	Stage 5
Unconsciously Incompetent	**Consciously Incompetent**	**Consciously Competent**	**Unconsciously Competent**	**Conscious Competence of Unconscious Incompetence**
"We don't know we have an issue"	"We recognize we need to do something"	"We are working on our DE&I efforts"	"DE&I is naturally how we think/act"	"We've mastered certain aspects of DE&I and can influence others."

Source: https://examinedexistence.com/the-four-states-of-competence-explained/

> "We should be willing to try things that haven't been tried before, then test, evaluate, iterate, and measure success to see if those things are working. Doing the same thing as others who have inconsistent results is not a best practice."
>
> – COURTNEY SIMMONS, Equity and Inclusion Director, Bell's Brewery, LLC

Devising Strategies

Organizations that excel at DE&I integrate it into their strategic plan. Many questions can be used to inform the development of a strategic plan. Examples of generic strategic planning questions are below:

1. Vision: Where do we want to be in 5-10 years?
2. Product and Service Scope: What products or services do we want to offer? What core competencies do we need?
3. Processes: What are our core processes? What needs transforming?
4. Scorecards: What indicators will we use to measure success?
5. Goals, Objectives, and Action Plans: How will we incrementally move toward our vision?

Source: An Overview of Strategic Planning by IRN, Inc. (John Cleveland)

Applying a DE&I Lens to Strategic Planning Questions

During the strategic planning process, applying a DE&I lens to each topic will help incorporate DE&I into the overall organizational plan. Compare the broad sample questions on the previous page to the focused sample questions below to get an idea of what this could look like.

Vision

Does our company's vision include a compelling case for DE&I? Is DE&I considered to be a means to growth and success?

Product and Service Scope

Do our products and services recognize diversity and accessibility from the onset of development? Do our products and services include research and product testing that measure how different groups and cultures may use the products and services? Are our products and services supported by ethnically or demographically diverse teams?

Processes

Have we reviewed our processes to identify where bias might occur? Have we implemented strategies to mitigate bias?

Scorecards

Are we tracking metrics, including diversity of our workforce, promotions, leadership teams, and board? Are we benchmarking against the community we operate in or serve?

Goals, Objectives, and Action Plans

Do we have SMART DE&I goals that are reviewed on a consistent basis? Are DE&I goals integrated with the overall organizational strategy?

Developing a Scorecard

Business leaders are driven by data. Conveying important metrics in a concise scorecard is a leading practice. The data your company tracks should directly align with your strategic goals.

At a minimum, scorecards generally track workforce demographic data at various levels. Companies often compare their internal workforce to the community served or the location where it is headquartered. For some employers, the goal is to have a workforce that mirrors the community served. For most employers, the goal is to positively improve over time until internal goals are met.

Many employers track the following categories by race, ethnicity, and gender:
- Workforce: full- and part-time employees
- Various levels of leadership: board, C-suite, vice presidents, directors, mid-level managers, and supervisors
- New hires: external candidates
- Promotions: advancing internal employees from one position to another that has a higher rank, higher pay scale, salary range, and increased responsibilities
- Turnover: number of separations per year, length of time employed, reason for separation

Depending on your industry sector, additional data may be tracked. For example, law firms track the demographics of their partners. Educational institutions track the demographics of faculty and students.

> "There is a balance in meeting people where they are and acknowledging that in many corporate spaces we aren't there yet. It's difficult to bring up a justice and equity-related perspective. This work requires finding and striking a better balance between business outcomes and business impact, and justice and equity, and demanding that we shift our perspective from counting people and thinking of diversity as a means to an end to really being deliberate about understanding what systems have been created that perpetuate inequity."
>
> – COURTNEY SIMMONS, Equity and Inclusion Director, Bell's Brewery, LLC

Measuring Inclusion

The scorecard example on the previous page offered various data points to track demographics. It is equally important to establish and track inclusion measures to assess your workplace culture, especially as organizations move toward hybrid work environments. No single measure or tool can sufficiently do this. Instead, consider incorporating a combination of both quantitative and qualitative measures. Qualitative inclusion measures could include employee attitudes, the human experience, and community involvement.

Attitudes

Employee attitudes are generally measured using a confidential survey tool. Surveys are the best option to quickly reach a large audience. Organizations can incorporate inclusion topics into an existing employee engagement/climate survey or create a separate inclusion survey. Providing a Likert scale of responses is a good way to quickly assess data. Open-ended questions are helpful for soliciting candid feedback and better understanding an individual's unique experience.

Your analytics team will need to determine which type of response is best for each statement or question.
- Sample responses for a Likert scale:
  - Definitely untrue, not very true, somewhat true, mostly true, definitely true
  - Extremely likely, somewhat likely, not likely
  - Never, sometimes, most of the time, all of the time
- When proposing close-ended questions that request a "yes" or "no" answer, offer a comment box to probe the respondent. For example, "If no, please explain".

SEEK EMPLOYEE FEEDBACK

Suggested sample questions and statements are included here to support the development of your survey:

Diversity
- √ (Insert company name) has clearly defined diversity and understands its meaning.
- √ (Insert company name) values diversity.
- √ Leadership understands that diversity is critical to our current and future organizational success.
- √ (Insert company name) invests time, energy, and resources into building diverse teams.
- √ I feel my unique background and identities (i.e. my differences) are valued at (insert company name).
- √ Managers at my organization are as diverse as the broader workforce.

Respect & Belonging
- √ (Insert company name) values inclusion.
- √ Employees at my organization respect and value each other's opinions and viewpoints.
- √ I feel welcome to express my true feelings at work.
- √ My voice and opinions are heard by leaders.
- √ I feel a sense of belonging and the people in my organization care about me.
- √ During the decision-making process, my ideas and suggestions are fairly considered by other team members.
- √ Employees at my organization who help the organization achieve its strategic objectives are recognized and rewarded fairly.

Career Growth

- ✓ I am provided mentorship and sponsorship opportunities.
- ✓ I feel supported in my career growth.
- ✓ The process for career advancement/promotion is transparent to all employees.
- ✓ (Insert company name) provides access to professional development that further emphasizes the role of DE&I in our work.
- ✓ Individuals with a variety of identities have equitable opportunities for advancement.

Identity

For a deeper level of insight, consider asking questions that directly correspond to various aspects of identity. These questions can be asked based on different identities such as gender, race/ethnicity, ability, religious beliefs, political ideology or affiliation, etc.

- ✓ As a _____ I feel welcome in my company/organization.
- ✓ As a _____ I am treated with respect by colleagues.
- ✓ As a _____ I am treated with respect by my supervisor.
- ✓ As a _____ I am treated with respect by subordinates.
- ✓ Policies and practices in my organization consider the needs of _____.
- ✓ _____ are provided adequate opportunities to participate in professional development that are relevant to _____ in this leadership, staff, etc.
- ✓ My organization provides services to address the needs of _____.
- ✓ I can openly express my religious/spiritual beliefs at work.

Employee Satisfaction & Retention

- ✓ I am happy in my current role.
- ✓ I enjoy the daily activities and responsibilities associated with my work.
- ✓ I receive open and honest communication from the organization.
- ✓ Share the top three (3) benefits of being an employee here.
- ✓ If you could change anything about the organization, what would it be?
- ✓ How likely are you to search for a new job?
- ✓ What can we do better to retain you as an employee?

Implementation

When determining the specific questions to ask and who to invite to participate, remember the survey process must be tailored to your specific industry and stakeholders. For example, in addition to surveying staff about the workplace culture, higher education institutions should also survey their students, faculty, and staff about how they experience campus.

When considering how to implement, focus on accessibility, a minimal time commitment from respondents, and ease of use for all employees. Inclusion surveys should be administered every year. Initially the data collected should be used to create a baseline measure of employee perceptions. Look for pockets of inconsistency and use the insights to identify areas for improvement and to take action. Measuring inclusion can help inform the creation of unique programs and initiatives that align with your organization's strategic goals.

When the data collection period is complete, share aggregate survey results and next steps with respondents. Employees who took time to submit a survey will want to know their opinions are leading to organizational change. Resurvey the same group to track changes in attitudes. Consistently assessing the data over time should also help indicate if you are moving the needle on inclusion.

The Human Experience

An individual's lived experience working for a company will look very different based on their own identities as well as their organizational dimensions of diversity (reference the Dimensions of Diversity wheel on page 34 for more). Other measures that some companies have linked to inclusion are listed below, along with questions to consider:

Development and Engagement

- **DE&I education:** What educational opportunities, trainings, workshops, or certifications have your organization made available to all employees regardless of role, shift worked, or location?

- **Professional development:** Do you offer mentorship and sponsorship programs? Are you tracking and reporting engagement and completion rates? Consider both quantity and demographics of participants served, with emphasis on historically underrepresented groups. What positive impact can be documented and shared?

- **Employee engagement:** Are you tracking absenteeism?

- **Chief Executive Officer (CEO) engagement:** Can you provide examples that demonstrate your CEO's commitment to DE&I? Are you seeking feedback on the perception of the CEO's leadership as a champion of DE&I?

Retention and Turnover

- **Retention:** Do you track employee retention? What is the average number of months or years an employee stays with your company? Does a specific group (gender, race, age, etc.) tend to separate more often than others?

- **Turnover:** Are you tracking turnover? Do you have a formula to calculate turnover? Have you estimated the cost of turnover for various roles in your organization?

- **Stay interviews:** Do you seek insight on what matters most to the employees you want to retain? Could include workstyles, benefits, management preferences, training opportunities, culture improvements, etc.

- **Exit interviews:** Are you hosting exit interviews? Do the questions link to inclusion?
    - Why did you decide to separate from the company?
    - How would you describe the company culture?
    - What could we have done differently to retain you?
    - In the future, would you ever consider returning to this company?
    - Did management play any role in your decision to separate?
    - Did the organization live up to your expectations based on the expressed DE&I statement, vision, goals, and values?

> "It is important that as D&I practitioners we assist organizations in understanding how essential inclusion is to foster an environment that is innovative and creative in regard to problem solving. Organizations that are committed to integrated D&I principles as part of their ethos tend to improve their retention and recruitment of talent."
>
> — CANDY S. MCCORKLE, PH.D.
> Vice President of Diversity & Inclusion
> Western Michigan University

Business Practices and Metrics

- **Policies, benefits, and initiatives:** Do the current policies, practices, programs, compensation, and benefits adequately support the needs of the varying identities of employees?

- **Productivity:** How has productivity changed over a designated period (individual, department level, or companywide)?

- **Profitability:** How has profitability changed over a designated period (individual, department, or companywide)?

- **Grievances:** Are you monitoring labor relations issues and complaints? Are you filtering the data by department, business unit, or role to gain a perspective on areas that need additional support?

If you do not have the interest or capacity to develop your own assessments tools, there are several vendors offering inclusion indexes. Some assessment tools are listed in the Appendix, page 68.

Community Involvement

Many organizations who prioritize DE&I also invest by supporting and advocating for DE&I topics and initiatives in the community, government, and society. Examples are below.

- **Corporate outreach:** Does the company utilize the full potential of employees, consumers, stakeholders, and experts as resources to meet DE&I goals?

- **Corporate social responsibility:** How does the company provide for the social and economic wellbeing of the diverse community it serves?

- **Supplier diversity:**
  - Does your company have a database of certified diverse vendors?
  - What percentage of your total spend is dedicated to purchasing from businesses that are owned by minorities, women, veterans, people with disabilities, or LGBTQ individuals?
  - What percentage of contractors reflect underrepresented groups?
  - Does your company have a formal supplier diversity program?
  - How is your company promoting the economic growth of marginalized groups?

- **Community service and engagement:**
  - Does the organization encourage employee volunteerism in community projects related to DE&I by providing time off or compensation?
  - In what ways does your organization engage with the surrounding community to support DE&I efforts?
  - What kind of events does your company volunteer at, promote, or sponsor?
  - What kind of organizations does your company partner with to advance inclusion and equity?
  - What is the total number of formal partnerships established? What impact have these partnerships made?
  - Does your company seek feedback from external stakeholders?
  - How are you measuring the qualitative impact of these community efforts?

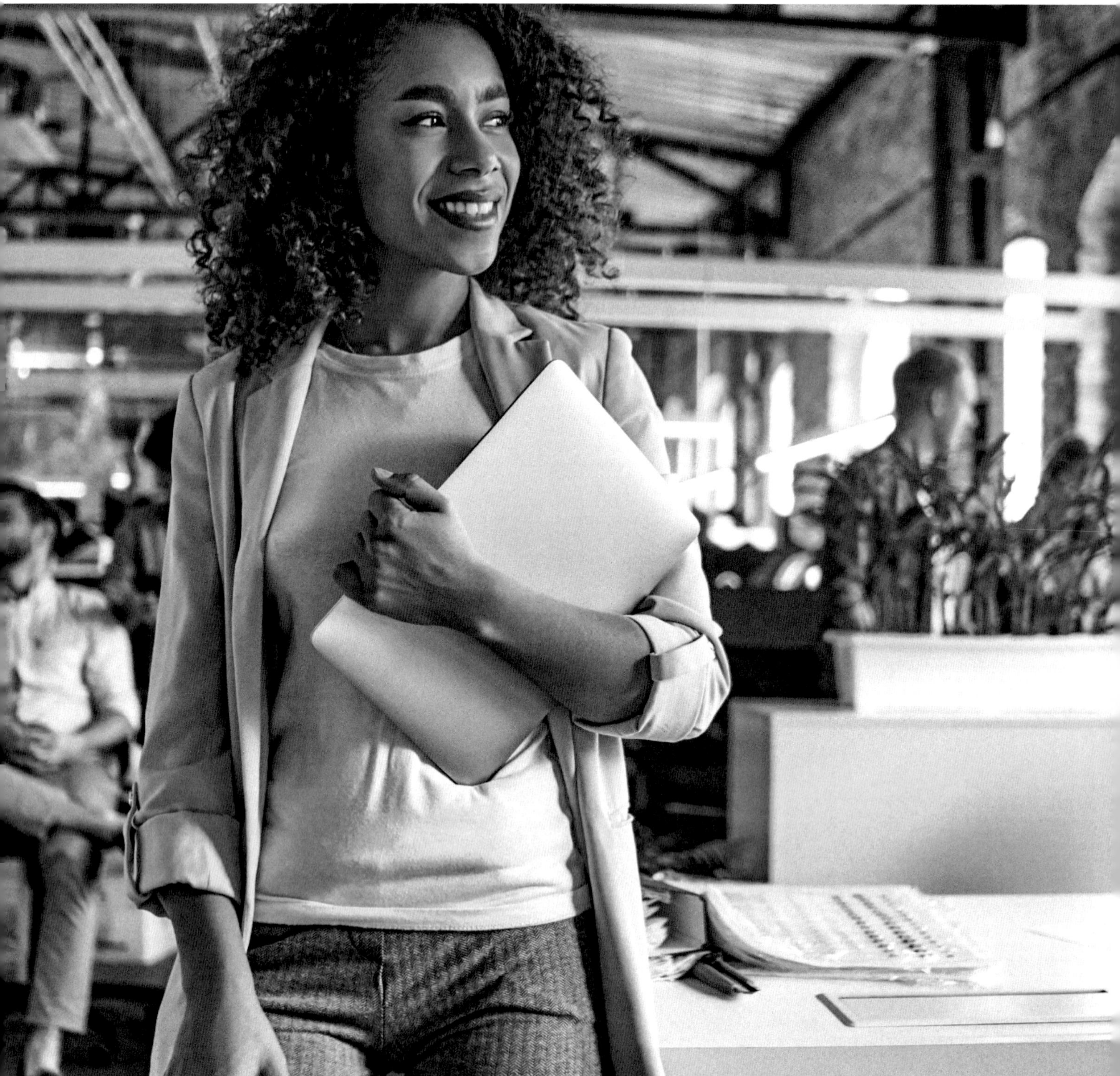

Competency 4:
Leading

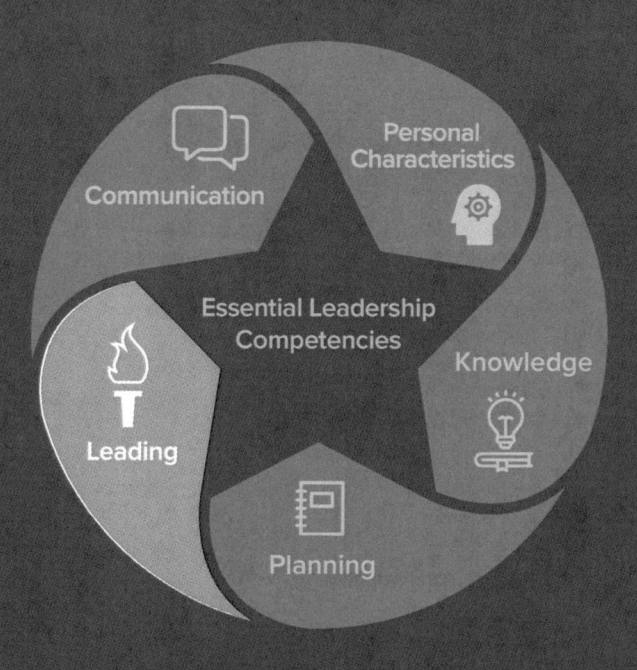

Leading organizational change requires both business acumen and political savvy to navigate an organization and communicate data to compel people to act. It also involves influence to shift mindsets, solve problems, and disrupt programs, practices, and systems to move the organization forward.

"When leading for equity, belonging and inclusion, we can't just focus on being responsive. Our leadership has to see beyond current urgent issues. Our concern must include dismantling the policies and systems that breed inequities. We must build structures, systems, policies, and protocols that foster a new way of relating and valuing others."

— BRANDY LOVELADY MITCHELL, ED.D., Director of Diversity, Equity, and Inclusion, Michigan Education Association

Leading Competencies

A DE&I officer's ability to lead is largely determined by the support of the President/CEO and the organizational infrastructure they have established. Strategies are most successful when the DE&I officer reports directly to the CEO. In addition to securing CEO-level support, an effective officer should be able to use their influence to gain followership, create shared accountability, and ultimately drive change.

Competency Statements	
An effective DE&I officer should ...	**Application**
1 Secure CEO-level support for DE&I	• Access to the CEO is critical • Includes transformative C-Suite and middle management leadership • President/CEO allows DE&I officer to "lead" and not just "manage" • President/CEO provides DE&I officer with "cover" or protection from resistant colleagues
2 Negotiate the needed level of autonomy to make change	• Secure the appropriate level of resources (financial and personnel) • Create shared responsibility to hold leaders accountable to metrics
3 Gain followership throughout various levels of the organization, beyond positional authority based on passion, competence, and credibility	• Help others see how inclusion and equity are the work of ALL, not just those who are underrepresented and/or marginalized • Navigate the organization using business acumen and political savvy • Identify and galvanize majority accomplices to move DE&I work forward • Move at a pace that is appropriate for the organization • Clearly and transparently communicate the plan, current status, and timelines • Connect with individual contributors across multiple levels of the organization • When applicable, leverage and collaborate with formal and informal team members to empower them and advance the work together
4 Consult and cooperate with various internal stakeholders to execute strategic plan	• Provide policy and procedure guidance across various departments to reduce bias and systems that perpetuate inequity • Critique policies and initiatives to ensure they align to DE&I strategy and amplify any and all portions that may be counterproductive • Support learning and organizational development teams with curriculum development and training delivery • Build a strong relationship with human resources and talent development • Engage with labor relations and unions for a variety of tasks, including but not limited to EEOC reporting, contract negotiation and grievances
5 Collaborate with community partners for sourcing, engagement, and philanthropy	• Be the lead voice, while equipping and empowering others to be voices of the organization's DE&I commitment in the community • Build relationships with high schools, intermediate school districts, community colleges, universities, non-profits, workforce development agencies, and foundations

"You can't have true CEO commitment if you don't have a dedicated leader, specifically at the executive level once an organization reaches a certain size. It is equivalent to saying, 'we don't need a CFO, it's everyone's responsibility to be fiscally responsible.' You need accountability, capability and expertise to gain traction. Otherwise it opens you up to more criticism." — ABE CARRILLO, Associate Vice President, Global Inclusion & Diversity, HDR INC.

CQ Knowledge for Leaders

Research by Global Leadership and Organizational Behavior Effectiveness (GLOBE) examines leaders and followers across 62 countries to determine similarities and differences in what followers want from their leaders.

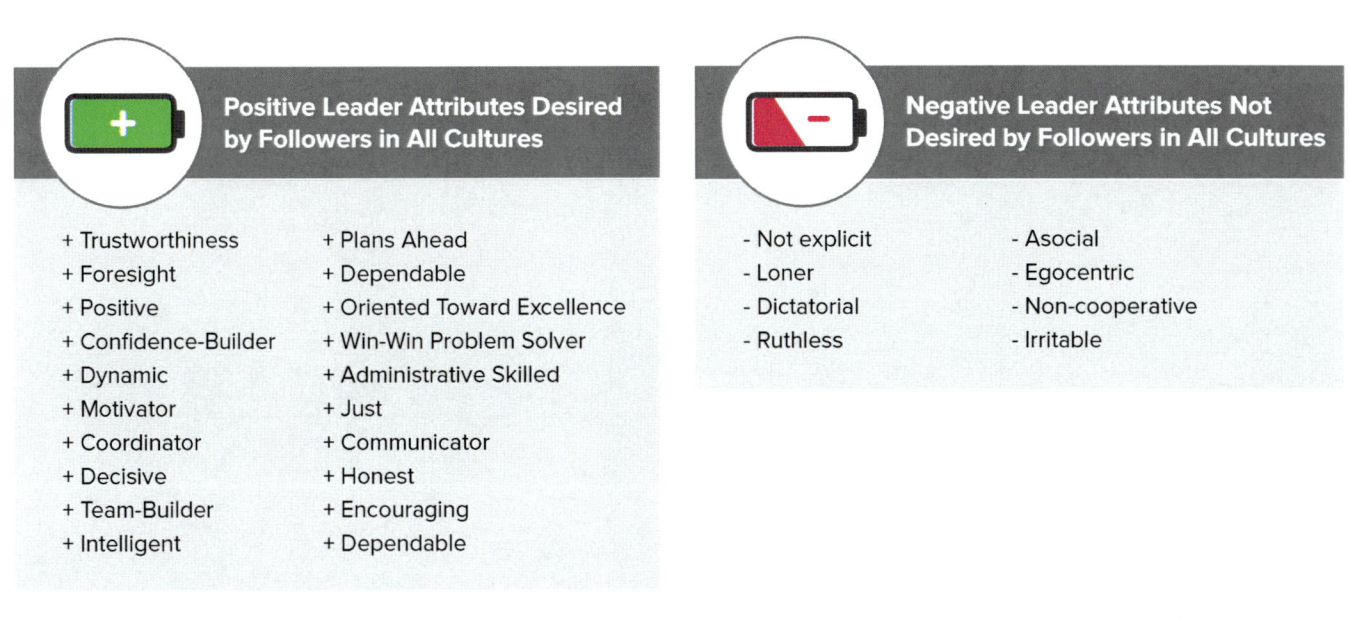

Positive Leader Attributes Desired by Followers in All Cultures

- + Trustworthiness
- + Foresight
- + Positive
- + Confidence-Builder
- + Dynamic
- + Motivator
- + Coordinator
- + Decisive
- + Team-Builder
- + Intelligent
- + Plans Ahead
- + Dependable
- + Oriented Toward Excellence
- + Win-Win Problem Solver
- + Administrative Skilled
- + Just
- + Communicator
- + Honest
- + Encouraging
- + Dependable

Negative Leader Attributes Not Desired by Followers in All Cultures

- - Not explicit
- - Loner
- - Dictatorial
- - Ruthless
- - Asocial
- - Egocentric
- - Non-cooperative
- - Irritable

Source: The Cultural Intelligence Center, What's your CQ? Participant Guide, 2020.

Credibility is Gained by:

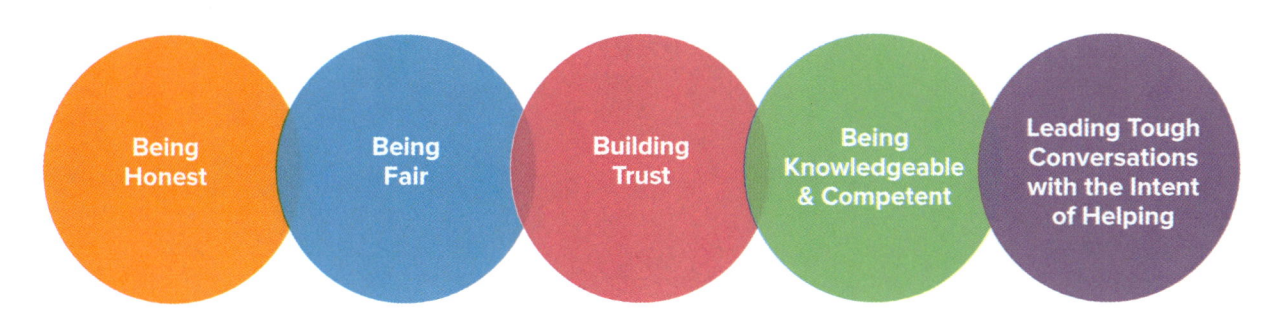

Being Honest → **Being Fair** → **Building Trust** → **Being Knowledgeable & Competent** → **Leading Tough Conversations with the Intent of Helping**

> "It's not impactful for one person (diversity officer) to tell others what needs to happen. You gain buy-in by bringing key stakeholders to the table. A great leader once told me that people support what they help to create."
>
> – DARIUS QUINN, Human Resources Manager and DEI Leader, Kent County

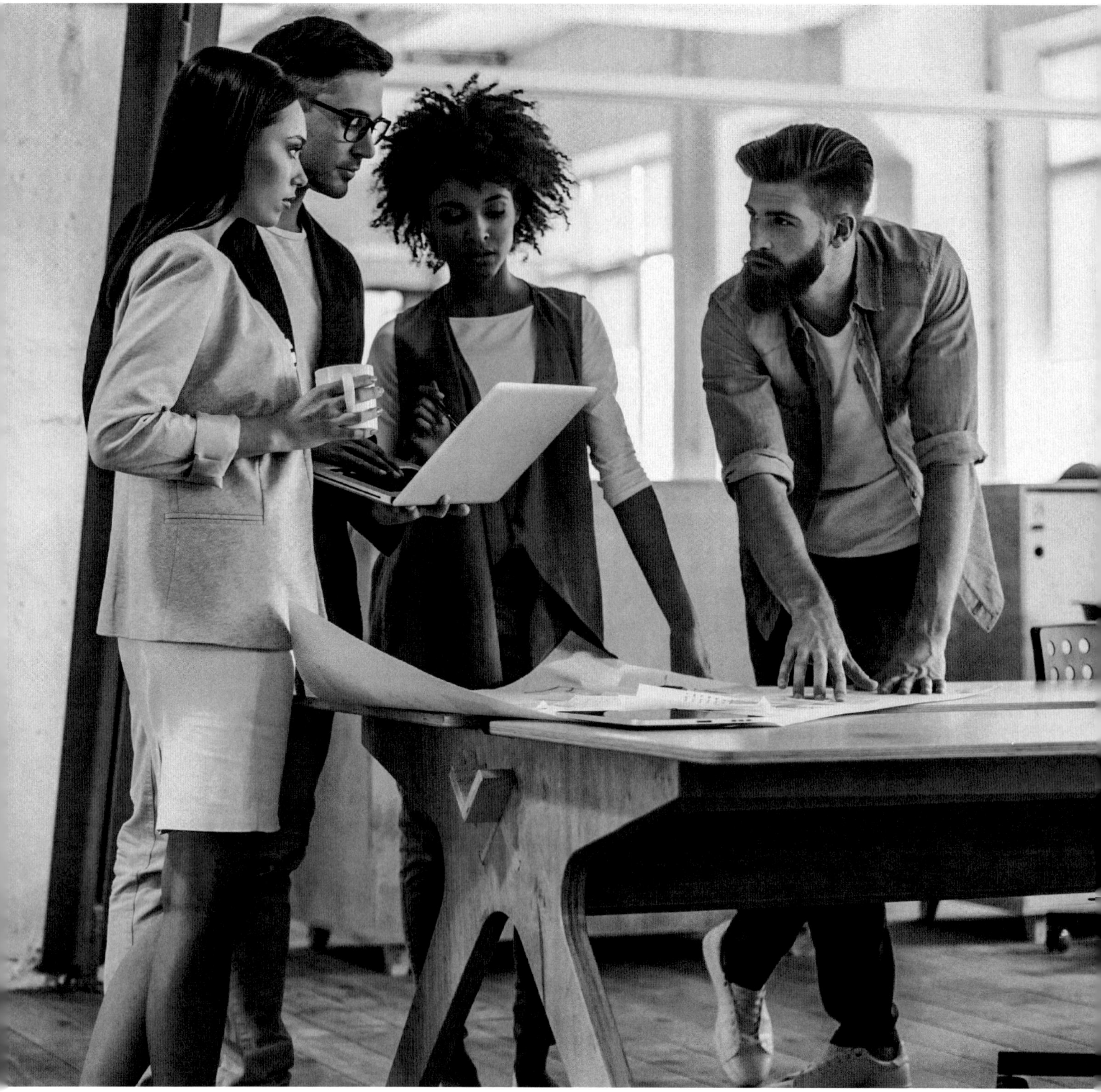

Competency 5:
Communication

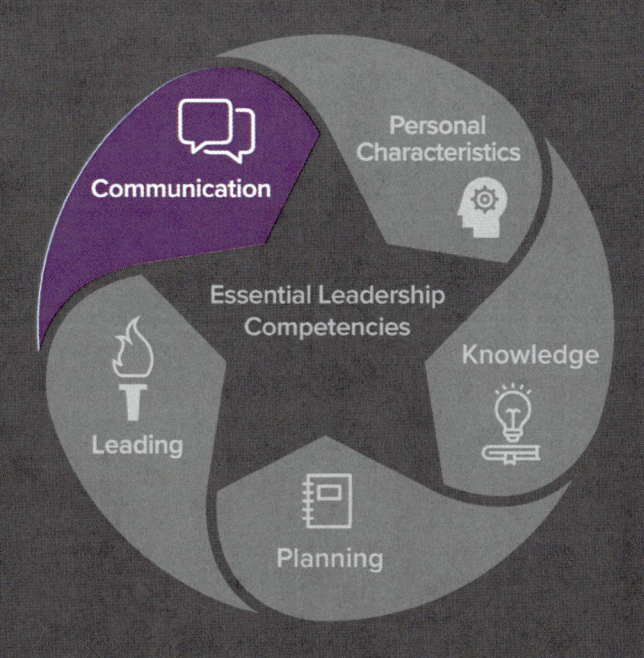

This competency includes listening to others to receive verbal information, speaking to others to convey verbal information; reading documents, charts, graphs, tables, forms, prose, and continuous text; and writing to convey or document written information.

Source: Talxcellenz. "Foundational Competency Definitions" Metrics Reporting (2020)

"It's critical for chief diversity officers to be able to connect the dots for others within their organization about how diversity, equity, and inclusion are related to the overall company mission as well as their specific roles."

— LATOYA BOOKER, Director of Diversity, Equity, and Inclusion, Davenport University

Communication Competencies

An effective DE&I officer needs to engage with a wide range of audiences on complex topics, and these subjects often are difficult to discuss. The competencies include being able to communicate in a tactful, professional, and compelling way; encouraging and mediating healthy discussions; and being creative to inspire and influence change.

Competency Statements

An effective DE&I officer should …	Application
1 Effectively communicate with tact and professionalism to multiple internal (C-suite to frontline employees) and external audiences	• Display proficient written and verbal communication skills • Utilize various channels to engage stakeholders and distribute information (social media, virtual platforms, internal and external web pages, blogs, short videos, emails, newsletters, annual reports, printed materials, etc.) • Adjust messaging and communication style to deliver content in a way that resonates with different stakeholders • Understand your audience, from a demographic and cultural perspective • Tailor message length, objectives, tone, data points, etc. for each scenario • Avoid assumptions about what a person knows or doesn't know, should or should not know
2 Articulate a compelling vision, business case, and moral case for diversity, equity, and inclusion as an organizational imperative	• Link diversity to other change management efforts, growth strategies, and sustainability plans • Define and communicate roles, responsibilities, and timelines • Clearly differentiate between diversity, equity, and inclusion. The business case must contain all
3 Facilitate bold and difficult conversations about race and other dimensions of diversity that also create a brave space for people to be pushed beyond their comfort zones, where they can be challenged respectfully, and where they are free to disagree	• Use dialogue to promote a sense of inclusion, welcoming, and belonging throughout various levels of the organization • Use language that calls people in, versus making them feel "less than," attacked, or villainized • Ask individuals for their preferred pronouns. Incorporate them into email signatures and various other forms of communication • Challenge status quo to reduce bias and advocate for more equitable opportunities
4 Use storytelling and other creative approaches to connect, inspire, educate, and influence	• Share personal experiences backed by data to help people connect to the subject without compromising the content • Gain buy-in and engage others in the work by connecting the DE&I concepts, principles, and strategies to their individual roles and the operational functions

> "Our goal is not to change people's minds but rather to crack their certainty – offering an alternate perspective."
>
> – COURTNEY SIMMONS, Equity and Inclusion Director, Bell's Brewery, LLC

How to Communicate with Impact

Effective communicators learn as much as they can about their audiences before initiating a conversation, walking into a meeting, or delivering a presentation. The tips below will help you understand your audience, craft a message, and deliver it with credibility.

Communication Tips

Audience	Message	Messenger	A Look of Credibility
• Attitudes • Number of attendees • Gender ratio • Age • Educational background • Job functions & expertise • Cultural orientation	• Organized & focused • Clear & concise points • Activating (persuasive, motivating, inspiring)	• Engaging & energized • Professional & prepared • Varied vocal tone • Good rate of delivery (speed) • Effective graphics • Prompting dialogue	• Sustained eye contact • Good posture • Purposeful, descriptive gestures • Professional dress & grooming

Source: Speak Up & Be Effective. Jennifer Maxson & Associates

Personality Assessments: A Communication Tool

Understanding the similarities and differences, as well as preferences and values of colleagues in your organization, can not only improve communication but also increase your team's productivity and performance.

Many employers rely on some variation of a personality assessment designed to help team members communicate and cooperate better. Three of the most common assessments are below:

Cultural Intelligence Center, Cultural Values Profile: This self-assessment can be used to describe an individual's personal preferences or cultural-value orientations based on the 10 largest cultural clusters in the world.

DiSC® Assessment: The DiSC model provides a common language that people can use to better understand themselves and adapt their behavior with others. DiSC profiles are designed to increase self-knowledge, including how participants respond to conflict, what motivates them or causes stress. Understanding the same perspectives about colleagues can help facilitate cooperation and communication.

Meyer-Briggs Type Indicator®: This commonly used tool is based on psychiatrist Carl Jung's theory that people experience the world four ways, through: sensation, intuition, feeling and thinking.

Each of these assessments is described in greater detail in the Appendix.

Part 4:
IMPROVING SKILLS

Self-assessments, reflection questions, and an action plan to improve DE&I leadership competencies.

Self-Assessment

During the self-assessment, the five important competencies (personal characteristics, knowledge, planning, leading, and communication) will be revisited. For each competency statement, please rate yourself on a scale of 1-5.

1 = Definitely Untrue | 2 = Not Very True | 3 = Somewhat True | 4 = Mostly True | 5 = Definitely True

Self-Assessment: Personal Characteristics

Competency Statements – I am:	Definitely Untrue	Not Very True	Somewhat True	Mostly True	Definitely True
1 Self-aware. I understand my own cultural influences, values, identities, triggers, dimensions of diversity and how I am situated within the organization, community and world.	1	2	3	4	5
2 Resilient. I continuously move forward while encountering obstacles and lack of support.	1	2	3	4	5
3 Authentic. I offer genuine and trustworthy leadership.	1	2	3	4	5
4 A catalyst. I spark or accelerate change within my organization.	1	2	3	4	5
5 Relationship-oriented. I foster meaningful partnerships with colleagues and community stakeholders.	1	2	3	4	5

Total
Add together all the numbers circled in rows 1-5 and place the sum in the box to the right.

Self-Assessment: Knowledge

Self-Rating: In each row below (numbered 1-5), circle the number that most accurately describes your skill set.

Competency Statements – I can:	Definitely Untrue	Not Very True	Somewhat True	Mostly True	Definitely True
1 Develop content knowledge that is critical to effective DE&I strategies.	1	2	3	4	5
2 Create personal knowledge networks.	1	2	3	4	5
3 Research DE&I standards and best practices, especially those that are relevant to my specific industry sector.	1	2	3	4	5
Total Add together all the numbers circled in rows 1-5 and place the sum in the box to the right.					

Self-Assessment: Planning

Self-Rating: In each row below (numbered 1-5), circle the number that most accurately describes your skill set.

Competency Statements – I can:	Definitely Untrue	Not Very True	Somewhat True	Mostly True	Definitely True
1 Use collaborative planning processes to integrate the organization's DE&I vision and tactics into the overall strategic plan.	1	2	3	4	5
2 Use data to assess the organization's current state and understand where the organization stands relative to its DE&I goals.	1	2	3	4	5
3 Design, implement and manage internal DE&I programs and initiatives (as needed).	1	2	3	4	5
4 Create a shared DE&I culture across the organization.	1	2	3	4	5
Total Add together all the numbers circled in rows 1-5 and place the sum in the box to the right.					

Self-Assessment: Leading

Self-Rating: In each row below (numbered 1-5), circle the number that most accurately describes your skill set.

Competency Statements – I can:	Definitely Untrue	Not Very True	Somewhat True	Mostly True	Definitely True
1 Secure CEO-level support for DE&I.	1	2	3	4	5
2 Negotiate the needed level of autonomy to make change.	1	2	3	4	5
3 Gain followership throughout various levels of the organization, beyond positional authority based on passion, competence, and credibility.	1	2	3	4	5
4 Consult and cooperate with various internal stakeholders to execute strategic plan.	1	2	3	4	5
5 Collaborate with community partners for sourcing, engagement, and philanthropy opportunities.	1	2	3	4	5
Total Add together all the numbers circled in rows 1-5 and place the sum in the box to the right.					

Self-Assessment: Communication

Competency Statements – I can:	Definitely Untrue	Not Very True	Somewhat True	Mostly True	Definitely True
Self-Rating: In each row below (numbered 1-5), circle the number that most accurately describes your skill set.					
1. Effectively communicate with tact and professionalism to multiple internal (C-suite to frontline employees) and external audiences.	1	2	3	4	5
2. Articulate a compelling vision, business case and moral case for diversity, equity, and inclusion as an organizational imperative.	1	2	3	4	5
3. Facilitate bold and difficult conversations about race and other dimensions of diversity that also create a brave space for people to be pushed beyond their comfort zones, where they can be challenged respectfully, and where they are free to disagree.	1	2	3	4	5
4. Use storytelling and other creative approaches to connect, inspire, educate, and influence.	1	2	3	4	5
Total Add together all the numbers circled in rows 1-5 and place the sum in the box to the right.					

Self-Assessment Scoresheet

Competency	Total Score for Designated Competency — Enter the totals calculated on the previous worksheets.
1. Personal Characteristics	
2. Knowledge	
3. Planning	
4. Leading	
5. Communication	

(Your highest scores can be interpreted as strengths; your lowest scores as areas to develop.)

Improving Skills | 61

Reflection

Now that you've completed the assessment and had a chance to review your results, please reflect on the five competencies and complete the worksheet below.

What are my strengths?

___

___

___

What are some areas I want to develop?

___

___

___

What are areas of opportunity? What are the three (3) most important things I should work on to strengthen my skillset?

___

___

___

What are some of my current challenges (personal or organizational)?

___

___

___

Further Examination of the Five Competencies

1 Personal Characteristics
  When reviewing the five essential personal characteristics competencies, which one resonated the most with you?

2 Knowledge
  Which dimensions of diversity may have been overlooked in the development of your DE&I programs?
  When reviewing the various DE&I topics, which two could you commit to spending more time learning about?

3 Planning
  When reviewing the 5 Stages of Competence model (page 41), where would you rate yourself as a leader? Where would you rate your organization?

4 Leading
  When looking at the Positive Leader Attributes (page 51), which traits do you currently exhibit? Where are there opportunities for improvement?

5 Communication
  Name one thing you could change to communicate with impact.

DE&I Competency Action Plan

Mark which of the five competencies you would like to improve:

○ Personal Characteristics   ○ Knowledge   ○ Planning   ○ Leading   ○ Communication

Personal Objective:

_____

_____

_____

Timeline: Start date _____   Frequency to review plan: ○ Weekly?   ○ Monthly?   ○ Quarterly?

Who will be your ally and accountability partner?

Name/title: _____   Organization: _____

Actions Necessary to Achieve Objective:

1. _____   4. _____

2. _____   5. _____

3. _____   6. _____

Stakeholders Needed to Engage:

1. _____   4. _____

2. _____   5. _____

3. _____   6. _____

Expected Outcomes:

1. _____

2. _____

3. _____

Conclusion

Effective leaders are essential to any organization's strategy to promote diversity, equity, and inclusion as a priority and move their company forward. At the same time, effective organizational strategies are needed for our entire region to create collective impact and a positive narrative.

Fortunately, the efforts to grow, encourage and promote competencies in this field do not have to happen in isolation. In fact, they cannot happen in isolation.

The West Michigan DE&I leaders who contributed to this guide have shared resources necessary to advance our region's maturation in this field of practice. Through the innovations they have developed at their organizations, they support our region's convergence around proven methods and tools to advance diversity, equity, and inclusion for all.

West Michigan Innovations And Recognitions

West Michigan employers are demonstrating their commitment to advancing DE&I. Some examples:

Calvin University

- Created a "Cognitive Error and Unconscious Bias" training module for all personnel searches. The module is required for every member of the search committee.

Davenport University

- For the past three years, the university's Diversity, Equity and Inclusion Council has placed in the Top 10 of the national Employee Resource Groups & Council Honors Awards (now known as the Diversity Impact Awards). Davenport is the only higher-education institution included.
- Received the INSIGHT Into Diversity Higher Education Excellence in Diversity Award for eight years.

Ernst & Young LLP (EY US)

- Recognized as No. 1 and inducted into *DiversityInc* magazine's Top 50 Hall of Fame in 2018, maintaining this status in 2019 and 2020. In 2020, recognitions included: No. 6 Top Companies for Supplier Diversity; No. 3 Top Companies for Employee Resource Groups; and Top Companies for LGBT Employees (no specific ranking).
- Named No. 1 on *Working Mother* magazine's 100 Best Companies list in 2020, its 24th year on the list and 15th consecutive year in the top 10. Named a Top 10 company on the 2020 Best Companies for Dads list for the third consecutive year. Additionally, named to *Working Mother's* Best Companies for Multicultural Women in 2020.
- Received a 100% rating on the Human Rights Campaign's Corporate Equality Index (CEI) for 2020. EY US has been designated as a "Best Place to Work for LGBT+ Equality since 2005.

Gentex Corp.
- The executive leadership team ratified the company's DEI Values in Action Statement.
- The DEI Council and Human Resources team members participated in an unconscious bias training to evaluate a potential pilot program for the company.
- The DEI Council found new community organizations with a diversity, equity, and inclusion focus to support through corporate sponsorship.

Grand Rapids Area Chamber of Commerce
- Observed and supported a positive trend in the business community around Diversity, Equity and Inclusion (DEI). Request for Implicit Bias trainings increased significantly, with the Chamber delivering over 20 trainings in the last six months of 2020. The Institute for Healing Racism workshops reached capacity. The annual DEI and Talent Summit had over 200 attendees participate virtually.

Grand Rapids Community College
- The Office of Diversity, Equity, and Inclusion facilitates a multi-year curriculum for faculty and staff. These opportunities provide employees with graduated stages of learning.

This project extends to students through teaching and service learning. In partnership with ODEI, the Center for Teaching Excellence and Instructional Support launched the Community of Practice (CoP) ImpACT grant. Faculty (adjunct and fulltime) recipients of the grant are provided with funding support to enhance equity practices. The grant's goal is to align with campus-wide efforts to shift the culture in classrooms and academic departments.

Grand Valley State University
- GVSU president appointed a campus-wide Network of Advisors for Racial Equity to ensure community shapes and commits to this work, and that Black faculty, staff, students, and alumni voices are elevated to the highest level of engagement with senior leaders.
- For more than 25 years, members of nine faculty and staff affinity groups have shared fellowship, connections to their cultural heritage and demonstrated positive impacts through mentorship. The groups are Asian Faculty and Staff Association, Black FSA, International Faculty and Friends, Interfaith Friendship Groups, Latino/a FSA, LGBT FSA, Native American Advisory Council, Positive Black Women and Women's Commission.
- One of five institutions nationally to be awarded the Seal of Excelencia, which recognizes institutions that intentionally serve Latino students and employees.

Herman Miller
- Designated Election Day as a holiday to ensure all employees have an opportunity to amplify their voices and participate in democracy with fewer barriers. Global employees will be granted a day of service.
- Signed on to CEO Action for Diversity & Inclusion and are sponsoring four employees for a full-time fellowship focused on Racial Equity.
- Invested in a learning partnership to complete training in 2020 with a focus on behaviors to mitigate bias and demonstrate inclusion, rooted in neuroscience.

Kent County
- As an equal opportunity employer, workforce demographics closely reflect the community it serves.
- Nearly 99% of 1,700 employees are trained in Cultural Intelligence.

Kent Intermediate School District
- Director of Diversity, Belonging, Equity & Inclusion (DBEI) shifted from Human Resources to the Superintendent's office as a declaration of this work being cross-cutting to the organization and region.

- For the first time, DBEI was a part of Kent ISD's onboarding of new staff. Nearly 100% of new staff has engaged in a Cultural Intelligence Assessment and Feedback group session.
- The Office of DBEI is offering a series of implicit bias and other capacity-building sessions for selection panels and hiring managers. All Secondary Programs staff have engaged in implicit bias training. The school board is engaging in racial equity training.

University of Michigan Health-West
- In first year (2019) of having an office dedicated to Diversity, Equity and Inclusion, DEI was approved as a key performance indicator in organization-wide Balanced Scorecard, helping align the DEI work of every department, ensuring accountability, measuring performance and communicating progress.

Ottawa County
- Established its first office of Diversity, Equity and Inclusion (DEI) and became fully staffed in June 2019, with a director and a support staff.
- Board of Commissioners proclaimed Jan. 22, 2019, as the National Day of Racial Healing.

Western Michigan University
- Created a Racial Justice Advisory Committee to identify, prioritize and recommend actions to address systemic racism and inequities on campus.
- WMU's president has created a $2 million fund called the Mountaintop Initiative to fund DEI efforts.

Reviewing Objectives

Each of these innovations reflect multiple aspects of the objectives set out at the beginning of this guide. These bear repeating here:

Leading Practices: Keys to DE&I Success
- Visible CEO commitment, leadership, support, and cover are critical
- An infrastructure must be in place that includes dedicated resources, data collection software, and shared accountability
- Intentionally embed DE&I into all functions of the organization
- Create SMART goals
- Use data and metrics to inform decision making, strategy, programs, and policies
- Remember that process and policy lead to sustainability
- Disrupt systems that perpetuate inequities
- Be curious and seek out learning opportunities
- Network with other DE&I practitioners including those who don't look like you
- Don't quit. Implement, test, pause, reflect, iterate, reroute but keep moving forward

Appendix

Sources Cited in Order of Appearance

Page 3
Vaughn, B.E. "The History of Diversity Training and its Pioneers." Strategic Diversity & Inclusion Management Magazine, Vol.1, Issue 1 (Spring 2007): 11-16.

https://diversityofficermagazine.com/diversity-inclusion/the-history-of-diversity-training-its-pioneers/#

Cleveland, John. "Field Building." Innovation Network for Communities (2007). www.in4c.net

Pages 5-6
Diversity Best Practices. "Glossary of Terms for Diversity, Equity, and Inclusion."

http://www.talent2025.org/uploads/files/DBP-glossary_of_terms_for_diversity_equity_inclusion_1.pdf

Livermore, David and Van Dyne, Linn. "Cultural Intelligence: The Essential Intelligence for the 21st Century." SHRM Foundation's Effective Practice Guidelines Series. (2015)

https://culturalq.com/wp-content/uploads/2016/05/SHRM-report.pdf

Sprout Social. "Inclusive language guidelines."

https://seeds.sproutsocial.com/writing/inclusive-language/

Page 16
Williams, Damon A. "Now is the Time: Developing a High Impact Diversity and Inclusion Infrastructure at the College of New Jersey." (2019)

https://diversity.tcnj.edu/wp-content/uploads/sites/113/2019/05/Damon-Williams-Report-FULL.pdf

Page 27
Brown, Jennifer. "How to be an Inclusive Leader: Your role in Creating Cultures of Belonging Where Everyone Can Thrive." (2019): 33, 38, 82.

Page 28
Ackerman, Courtney E. "Big Five Personality Traits: The OCEAN Model Explained." (2020)

https://positivepsychology.com/big-five-personality-theory/

Page 36
Wood, Jennifer M. "20 Cognitive Biases that Affect Your Decision Making." Mental Floss. (2015).

https://www.mentalfloss.com/article/68705/20-cognitive-biases-affect-your-decisions

Page 37
Worthington, R.L., Stanley, C.A, Smith, D.G. (2020). "Advancing the professionalization of diversity officers in higher education: Report of the Presidential Task Force on the Revision of the NADOHE Standards of Professional Practice." Journal of Diversity in Higher Education, 13, 1-22

https://nadohe.memberclicks.net/assets/2020SPPI/NADOHE%20Standards%202.0.pdf

Page 41
Examined Existence. "The Four States of Competence"

https://examinedexistence.com/the-four-states-of-competence-explained/

Page 42
Cleveland, John. An Overview of Strategic Planning. IRN, Inc.

Page 51
The Cultural Intelligence Center. "What's your CQ?" Participant Guide (2018): 24.

Page 53
Talxcellenz. "Foundational Competency Definitions" Metrics Reporting (2020)

Page 55
Jennifer Maxson & Associates. "Speak Up & Be Effective." (2019)

Additional Resources

Certification Programs

- Cornell University. Diversity and Inclusion Certificate: https://www.ecornell.com/certificates/
- Howard University School of Business. Executive Certification in Diversity Coaching: https://executive.coachdiversity.com/
- Institute of Diversity Certification. Certified Diversity Professional (CDP) or Certified Diversity Executive (CDE): https://www.diversitycertification.org/
- The Cultural Intelligence Center. CQ Certification: https://culturalq.com/products-services/certification/
- AIRS Powered by ADP. Certified Diversity and Inclusion Recruiter (CDR): https://airsdirectory.com/collections/certifications/products/certified-diversity-and-inclusion-recruiter-11-0-cdr
- Michigan State University. Diversity Assessment and Engagement Program: https://engage.msu.edu/about/projects/community-and-economic-development/diversity-assessment-and-engagement-program-daep
- Society for Human Resource Management. Inclusive Workplace Culture Specialty Credential: https://store.shrm.org/SHRMInclusive-Workplace-Culture-Specialty-Credential
- The Professionals Forum LLC – 2b Inclusive Diversity Leadership Academy: https://www.theprosforum.com/diversity-leadership-academy

Organizations and Associations

- Diversity Inc.: https://www.diversityinc.com/
- Diversity Best Practices: https://www.diversitybestpractices.com/
- Catalyst: https://www.catalyst.org/
- Society for Human Resource Management (SHRM): https://www.shrm.org/
- National Equity Project: https://nationalequityproject.org/
- West Michigan Chambers of Commerce:
  - Grand Rapids Area Chamber of Commerce – DE&I Services: https://www.grandrapids.org/diversity-services/
  - Michigan West Coast Chamber: https://www.westcoastchamber.org/
  - Muskegon Lakeshore Chamber: https://www.muskegon.org/
- Forum for Workplace Inclusion: https://forumworkplaceinclusion.org/
- Gallup DE&I: https://www.gallup.com/workplace/215939/diversity-inclusion.aspx
- Association of ERGs & Councils: https://www.ergcouncil.com/
- Intercultural Communications Institute: https://intercultural.org/
- Democracy Collaborative: https://democracycollaborative.org/
- The Society for Diversity: https://www.societyfordiversity.org/
- National Association of Diversity Officers in Higher Education: https://www.nadohe.org/standards-of-professional-practice-for-chief-diversity-officers
- Gartner Diversity, Equity, and Inclusion Resource Center: https://www.gartner.com/en/human-resources/insights/diversity-equity-inclusion

Assessments

- Intercultural Development Inventory (IDI): https://idiinventory.com/generalinformation/the-intercultural-development-continuum-idc/
- Gallup Inclusion Index: https://www.gallup.com/home.aspx
- DDI – Leadership Development and Assessment: https://www.ddiworld.com/
- Inclusive Leader Assessment: https://jenniferbrownspeaks.com/inclusive-leader-book/assessment/#jump_trgt
- DiSC®: https://www.discprofile.com/what-is-disc/overview
- National Diversity Council – NDC Index: http://ndcindex.org/
- Insight: Viewfinder – Campus Climate Surveys: https://campusclimatesurveys.com/
- HEDS, Diversity and Equity Campus Climate Survey: https://www.hedsconsortium.org/heds-diversity-equity-campus-climate-survey/

Reports and Leading Practices

- Russell Reynolds Associates. "A Leader's Guide: Finding and Keeping Your Next Chief Diversity Officer." (2018) http://www.talent2025.org/uploads/files/Chief-Diversity-Officer_1218_FINAL.pdf
- Deloitte. "Leadership Capability Modeling: Introducing the Next-generation competency model." https://www2.deloitte.com/content/dam/Deloitte/us/Documents/human-capital/us-leadership-capability-modeling.pdf

- O'Mara, Julie & Richter, Alan. The Centre for Global Inclusion. "Global Diversity & Inclusion Benchmarks: Standards for Organizations Around the World." (2017 Edition) http://www.talent2025.org/uploads/files/GDIB-V.090517.pdf
- Powell, John A., Menendian, Stephen, & Ake, Wendy. "Targeted Universalism Policy and Practice." Haas Institute for a Fair and Inclusive Society. (May 2019) https://haasinstitute.berkeley.edu/sites/default/files/targeted_universalism_primer.pdf
- Blackwell, Angela, Kramer, Mark, Vaidyanathan, Lalitha, Iyer, Lakshmi, & Kirschenbaum, Josh. "The Competitive Advantage of Racial Equity." Policy Link http://www.talent2025.org/uploads/files/The-Competitive-Advantage-of-Racial-Equity-final.pdf
- Talent 2025. PIVOT DE&I Employer Toolkit: http://www.talent2025.org/resources/pivot
- Inner City Insights. "Anchor Institutions and Urban Economic Development: From Community Benefit to Shared Value." Volume 1, Issue 2. (June 2011) http://www.talent2025.org/uploads/files/ICIC_Anchors-and-Urban-Econ-Dev.pdf
- Michigan Department of Civil Rights. Racial Equity Toolkit: https://www.michigan.gov/mdcr/0,4613,7-138-87162-472680--,00.html
- The Equity Book: Equity Toolkit. https://theequitybook.com/equity-toolkit/

Books to Build Your Knowledge

Bias
- Blindspot: Hidden Biases of Good People. Mahzarin R. Banaji and Anthony G. Greenwald.
- The Person You Mean to Be: How Good People Fight Bias. Dolly Chugh and Laszlo Bock.
- The Leader's Guide to Unconscious Bias: How to Reframe Bias, Cultivate Connection, and Create High-Performing Teams. Pamela Fuller & Mark Murphy with Anne Chow.
- Thinking, Fast and Slow. Daniel Kahneman

Inclusion
- Belonging at Work: Everyday Actions You Can Take to Cultivate an Inclusive Organization. Rhodes Perry, MPA.
- Inclusion: Diversity, The New Workplace & The Will to Change. Jennifer Brown.
- How to Be an Inclusive Leader: Your Role in Creating Cultures of Belonging Where Everyone Can Thrive. Jennifer Brown.
- The Inclusion Paradox: The Post Obama Era and the Transformation of Global Diversity (3rd Edition). Andrés T. Tapia.
- The Inclusion Dividend: Why Investing in Diversity & Inclusion Pays Off. Mason Donovan and Mark Kaplan.
- The Diversity Bonus: How Great Teams Pay Off in the Knowledge Economy. Scott E. Page.
- 101 Ways to Enjoy the Mosaic: Creating a Diverse Community Right in Your Own Backyard. Skot Welch.
- Women, Minorities, & Other Extraordinary People. Barbara B. Adams, PsyD.
- Lean In: Women, Work, and the Will to Lead. Sheryl Sandberg.
- Dirty Diversity: A Practical Guide to Foster an Equitable and Inclusive Workplace for All. Janice Gassam.

Workplace
- Giving Notice: Why the Best and the Brightest Leave the Workplace and How You Can Help Them Stay. Freada Kapor Klein.
- Diversity Resistance in Organizations. Kecia Thomas.
- Embracing the Value of Diverse Conversations: Finding Common Ground (3rd Edition). Eric M. Ellis M.A.
- Hidden Rules of Class at Work: Why You Don't Get Promoted. Ruby K. Payne, Ph.D. and Don L. Krabill.
- Better Allies: Everyday Actions to Create Inclusive, Engaging Workplaces. Karen Caitlin.
- The Chief Diversity Officer: Strategy, Structure, and Change Management. Damon A. Williams.
- Strategic Diversity Leadership: Activating Change and Transformation in Higher Education. Damon A. Williams.
- Equity: How to design organizations where everyone thrives. Minal Bopaiah.
- The Diversity Playbook. Dr. Michelle R. Loyd-Paige and Michelle D. Williams.

Cultural Intelligence and Cultural Competency

- Driven by Difference: How Great Companies Fuel Innovation Through Diversity. David Livermore.
- Leading with Cultural Intelligence: The Real Secret to Success. David Livermore.
- The Cultural Intelligence Difference: Master the One Skill You Can't Do Without in Today's Global Economy. David Livermore.
- Expand Your Borders: Discover 10 Cultural Clusters. David Livermore.

Race, Racism and Civil Rights

- Race, Work, and Leadership: New Perspectives on the Black Experience. Laura Morgan Roberts & Anthony J. Mayo.
- Uprooting Racism: How White People Can Work for Racial Justice (4th Edition). Paul Kivel.
- How to be an Antiracist. Ibram X. Kendi.
- Stamped from the Beginning: The Definitive History of Racist Ideas in America. Ibram X. Kendi.
- White Fragility: Why it's so hard for white people to talk about racism. Robin Diangelo.
- The New Jim Crow: Mass Incarceration in the Age of Colorblindness. Michelle Alexander.
- Covering: The Hidden Assault on Our Civil Rights. Kenji Yoshino.
- Post Traumatic Slave Syndrome: America's Legacy of Enduring Injury and Healing. Dr. Joy DeGruy.
- My Grandmother's Hands: Racialized Trauma and the Pathway to Mending Our Hearts and Bodies. Resmaa Menakem.
- The Sum of Us: What Racism Costs Everyone and How We Can Prosper Together. Heather McGhee and Random House Audio.
- White Rage: The Unspoken Truth of Our Racial Divide. Carol Anderson & Pamela Gibson.
- Waking Up White and Finding Myself in the Story of Race. Debbie Irving.
- Caste: The Origins of Our Discontents. Isabel Wilkerson and Robin Miles.
- The Color of Law: A Forgotten History of How our Government Segregated America by Richard Rothstein.
- Sisters of the Academy: Emergent Black Women Scholars in Higher Education by Anna Lucille Green, Reitumetse Obakeng Maboketa.
- Conversations in Black by Edward Gordon.
- Race Talk and the Conspiracy of Silence: Understanding and Facilitating Difficult Dialogues on Race by Derald Wing Sue.
- The Emperor Has No Clothes: Teaching about Race and Racism to People Who Don't Want to Know by Tema Jon Okun.
- The Possessive Investment in Whiteness: How White People Profit from Identity Politics by George Lipsitz.
- Understanding and Dismantling Racism: The Twenty-First Century Challenge to White America by Joseph Barndt.
- Why are all the Black Kids Sitting Together in the Cafeteria? And other Conversations about Race by Beverly Daniel Tatum.
- How Jews Became White Folks and What That Says About Race in America by Karen Brodkin.
- White Like Me: Reflections on Race from a Privileged Son by Tim Wise.
- Feeling White: Whiteness, Emotionality and Education by Cheryl E. Matias.
- For White Folks Who Teach in the Hood...and the Rest of Y'all Too: Reality Pedagogy and Urban Education by Christopher Emdin.
- America's Original Sin: Racism, White Privilege, and the Bridge to a New America by Jim Wallis.
- The 1619 Project. Nikole Hannah-Jones and The New York Times Magazine.
- Medical Apartheid by Harriet A. Washington.

Personality Assessments

Cultural Values Profile

This model by the Cultural Intelligence Center examines the different values and perspectives that emerge from a person's cultural differences.

The assessment provides feedback on 10 cultural value dimensions: individualism vs. collectivism; low power distance vs. high power distance; low uncertainty avoidance vs. high uncertainty avoidance; cooperative vs. competitive; short term vs. long term perspectives; direct vs. indirect communication; being vs. doing; universalism vs. particularism; non-expressive vs. expressive; and linear vs. non-linear approach to tasks. Find out more: https://culturalq.com/products-services/assessments/cultural-values-profile

DISC®

After completing a DiSC profile, participants receive a detailed report explaining where they fall on the continuum of four reference points:

- Dominance – emphasis on accomplishing results, the bottom line, confidence
- Influence – emphasis on influencing or persuading others, openness, relationships
- Steadiness – emphasis on cooperation, sincerity, dependability
- Conscientiousness – emphasis on quality and accuracy, expertise, competency

In addition to receiving a self-assessment, participants gain insights into dealing with other personality types on their team. Find out more: https://www.discprofile.com/what-is-disc

Meyer-Briggs®

The Meyer-Briggs Type Indicator® identifies basic preferences of four dichotomies in C.G. Jung's theory of psychological types.

These types lend themselves to the four-letter combinations used to define personalities: Extraversion (E) vs. Introversion (I), Sensing (S) vs. Intuition (N), Thinking (T) vs. Feeling (F), and Judging (J) vs. Perceiving (P).

The basis of the theory is that "seemingly random variation in the behavior is actually quite orderly and consistent, being due to basic differences in the ways individuals prefer to use their perception and judgment." (https://www.myers-briggs.org/my-mbti-personality-type/mbti-basics/)

Understanding preferences can help individuals grow professionally and help organizations become more effective.

MBTI offers a certification program to equip individuals with the essential information to deliver the instrument and provide feedback to recipients. Find out more: https://www.myersbriggs.org/

Thought Leaders

Effective DE&I officers seek to learn from others in the field who are succeeding. This is essential to developing DE&I as a field of practice. Following are some individuals considered to be leaders in the field. Some are authors, others are noted speakers. However, this is not intended to be all-inclusive and practitioners should seek out thought leaders whose ideas resonate for the continuous journey of diversity, equity, and inclusion.

- Kyler Broadus, Global Human Rights Activist, Lawyer, Business Law Professor
- Jennifer Brown, President and CEO, Jennifer Brown Consulting and Best-Selling Author, Inclusion: Diversity, the New Workplace and the Will to Change
- Joel Brown, Ed.D., Chief Visionary Officer, Pneumos
- Ashley Brundage, Vice President, Diversity and Inclusion, PNC Bank
- Dre Domingue, Ed.D., Assistant Dean of Students for Diversity and Inclusion, Davidson College
- Ben Duncan, Chief Diversity and Equity Officer, Multnomah County Office of Diversity and Equity
- Rhodes Perry, MPA, Founder and CEO, Rhodes Perry Consulting, LLC, best-selling author and host of The Out Entrepreneur podcast
- Robert Rodriguez, Ph.D., President, DRR Advisors LLC
- Steve Robbins, Ph.D., Founder of S.L. Robbins and Associates, Speaker, Author, Inclusion and Belonging Consultant
- Tim Wise, American Activist and author

Made in the USA
Monee, IL
19 October 2023